T0053031

INVENTIONS AND DISCOVERY

LOUIS PASTEUR and PASTEURIZATION

by Jennifer Fandel

illustrated by Keith Wilson, Rodney Ramos, and Charles Barnett III

Consultant:
Harry W. Paul
Professor Emeritus of History
University of Florida
Gainesville, Florida

Capstone

Mankato, Minnesota

Graphic Library is published by Capstone Press,
1710 Roe Crest Drive, North Mankato, Minnesota 56003.
www.capstonepub.com

Copyright © 2007 by Capstone Press, a Capstone imprint. All rights reserved.
No part of this publication may be reproduced in whole or in part, or stored in a
retrieval system, or transmitted in any form or by any means, electronic, mechanical,
photocopying, recording, or otherwise, without written permission of the publisher.
For information regarding permission, write to Capstone Press,
1710 Roe Crest Drive, North Mankato, Minnesota 56003.

Library of Congress Cataloging-in-Publication Data
Fandel, Jennifer.
    Louis Pasteur and pasteurization / by Jennifer Fandel; illustrated by Keith Wilson,
Rodney Ramos, and Charles Barnett III.
    p. cm.—(Graphic library: Inventions and discovery)
    Includes bibliographical references and index.
    ISBN-13: 978-0-7368-6844-0 (hardcover)
    ISBN-10: 0-7368-6844-5 (hardcover)
    ISBN-13: 978-0-7368-7896-8 (softcover pbk.)
    ISBN-10: 0-7368-7896-3 (softcover pbk.)
    1. Pasteur, Louis, 1822–1895—Comic books, strips, etc. 2. Microbiologists—France—
Biography—Comic books, strips, etc. 3. Food—Pasteurization—Comic books, strips, etc. I.
Wilson, Keith, 1936– ill. II. Ramos, Rodney, ill. III. Barnett, Charles, III ill. IV. Title. V. Series.
QR31.P37F36 2007
579.092—dc22
[B]   2006031540

Summary: In graphic novel format, tells the story of Louis Pasteur's invention of the
    pasteurization process and the effects of this invention on the spread of disease
    through food.

Designer	*Colorist*
Alison Thiele	Tami Collins
Storyboard Artist	*Editor*
Ron Frenz	Gillia Olson

Editor's note: Direct quotations from primary sources are indicated by a yellow background.

Direct quotations appear on the following pages:

Page 10, from the Oxford Dictionary of Quotations (New York: Oxford University Press, 1999).
Page 11, quoted in *Louis Pasteur* by Patrice Debre (Baltimore: Johns Hopkins University
    Press, 1998).

TABLE OF CONTENTS

CHAPTER 1
HAZARDOUS FOOD

In the mid-1800s, people didn't know that germs cause disease. They knew microorganisms existed, but they were believed to be harmless. Because no one knew that germs cause disease, no one knew how diseases spread.

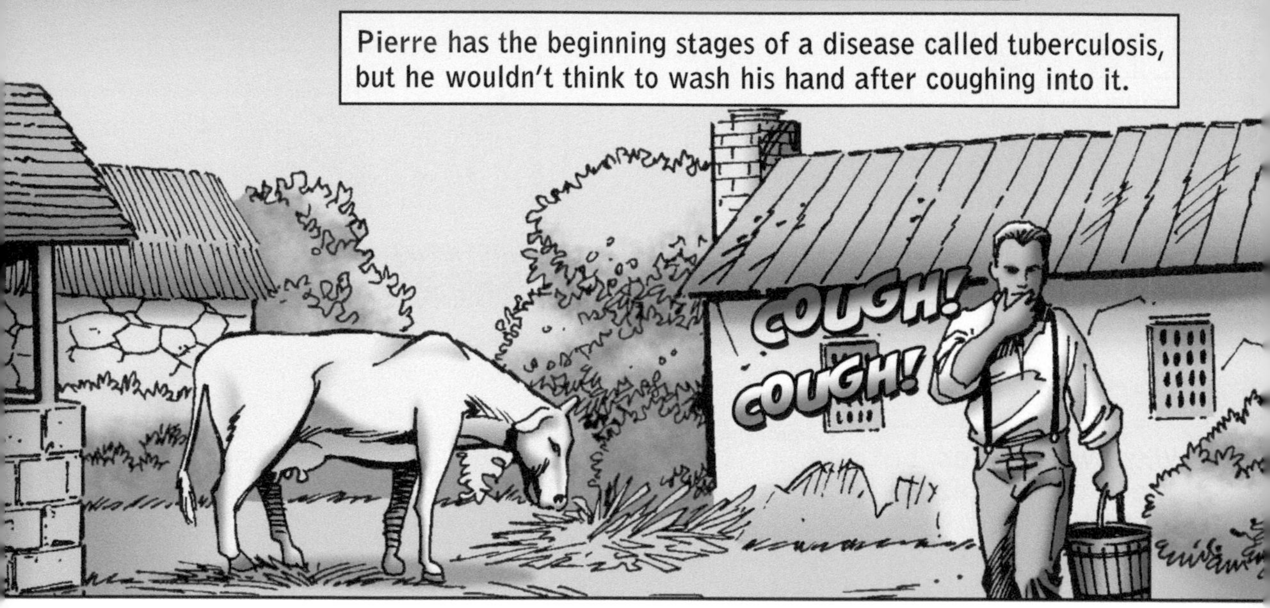
Pierre has the beginning stages of a disease called tuberculosis, but he wouldn't think to wash his hand after coughing into it.
COUGH!
COUGH!

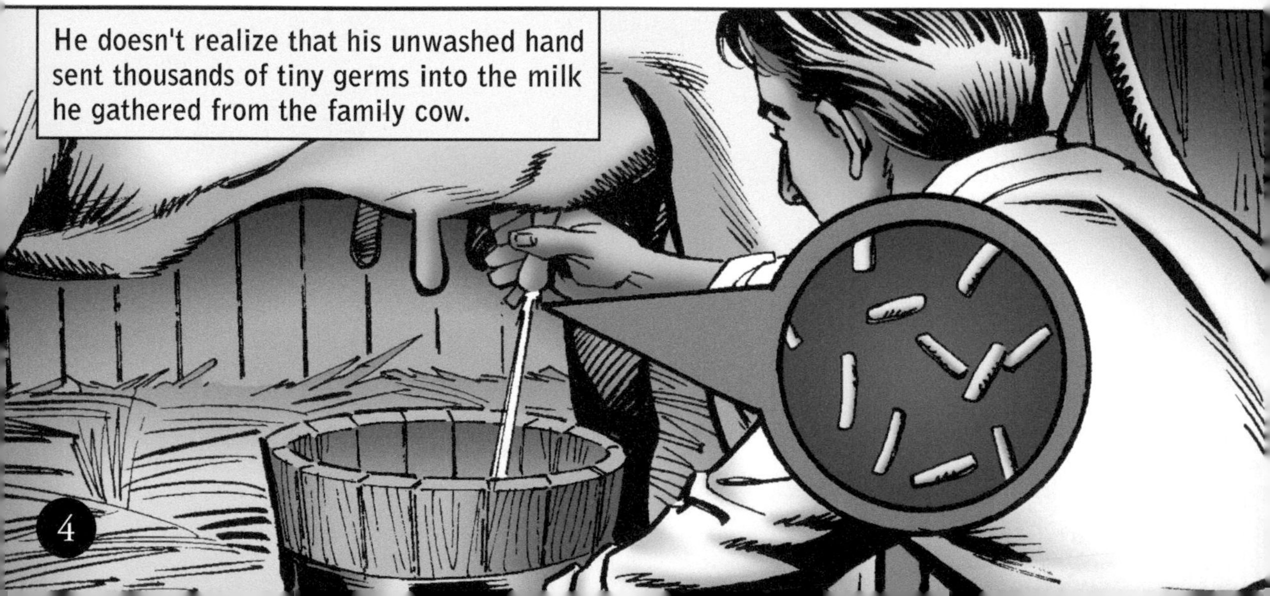
He doesn't realize that his unwashed hand sent thousands of tiny germs into the milk he gathered from the family cow.

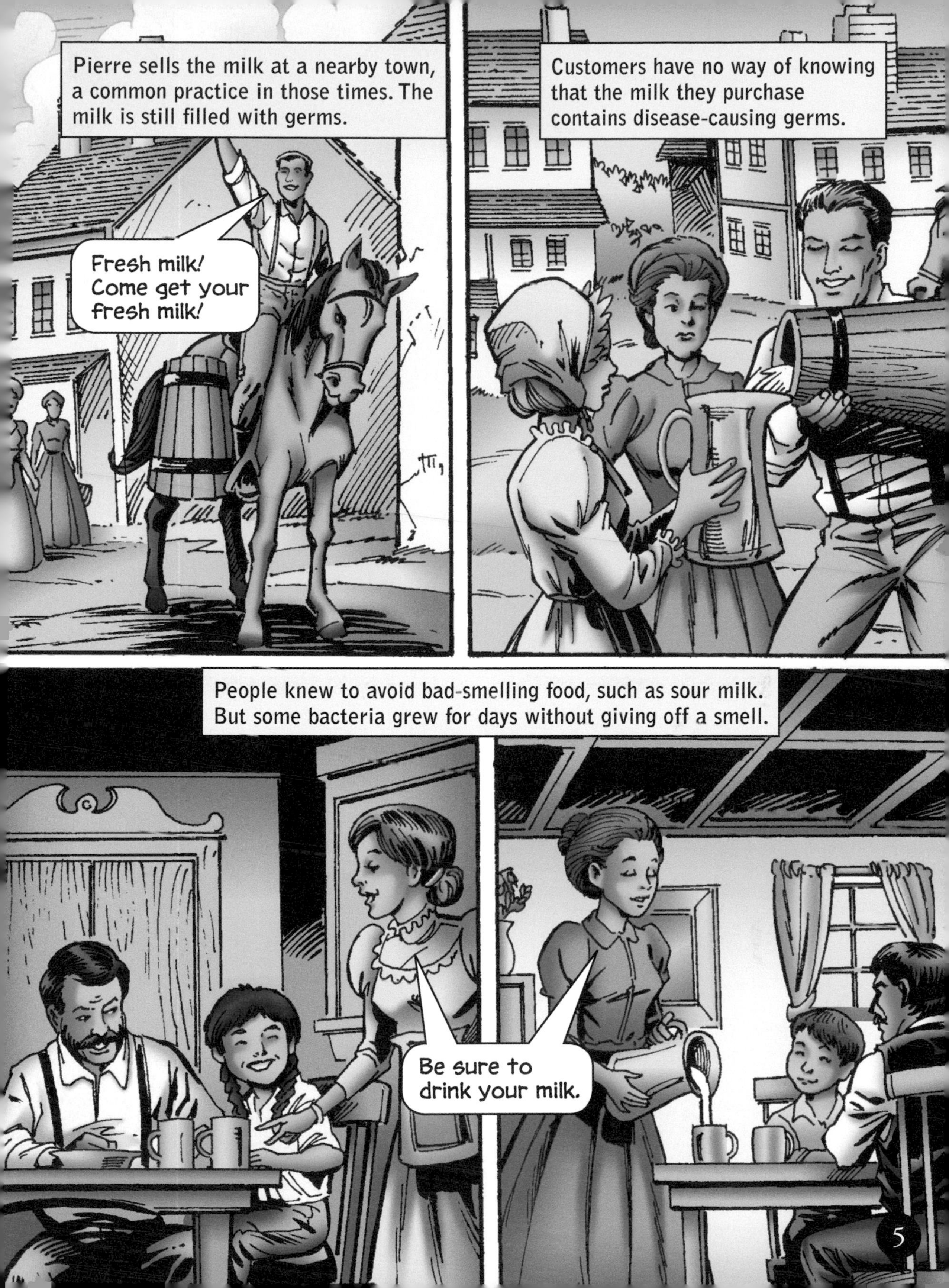
Pierre sells the milk at a nearby town, a common practice in those times. The milk is still filled with germs.
Fresh milk! Come get your fresh milk!
Customers have no way of knowing that the milk they purchase contains disease-causing germs.
People knew to avoid bad-smelling food, such as sour milk. But some bacteria grew for days without giving off a smell.
Be sure to drink your milk.

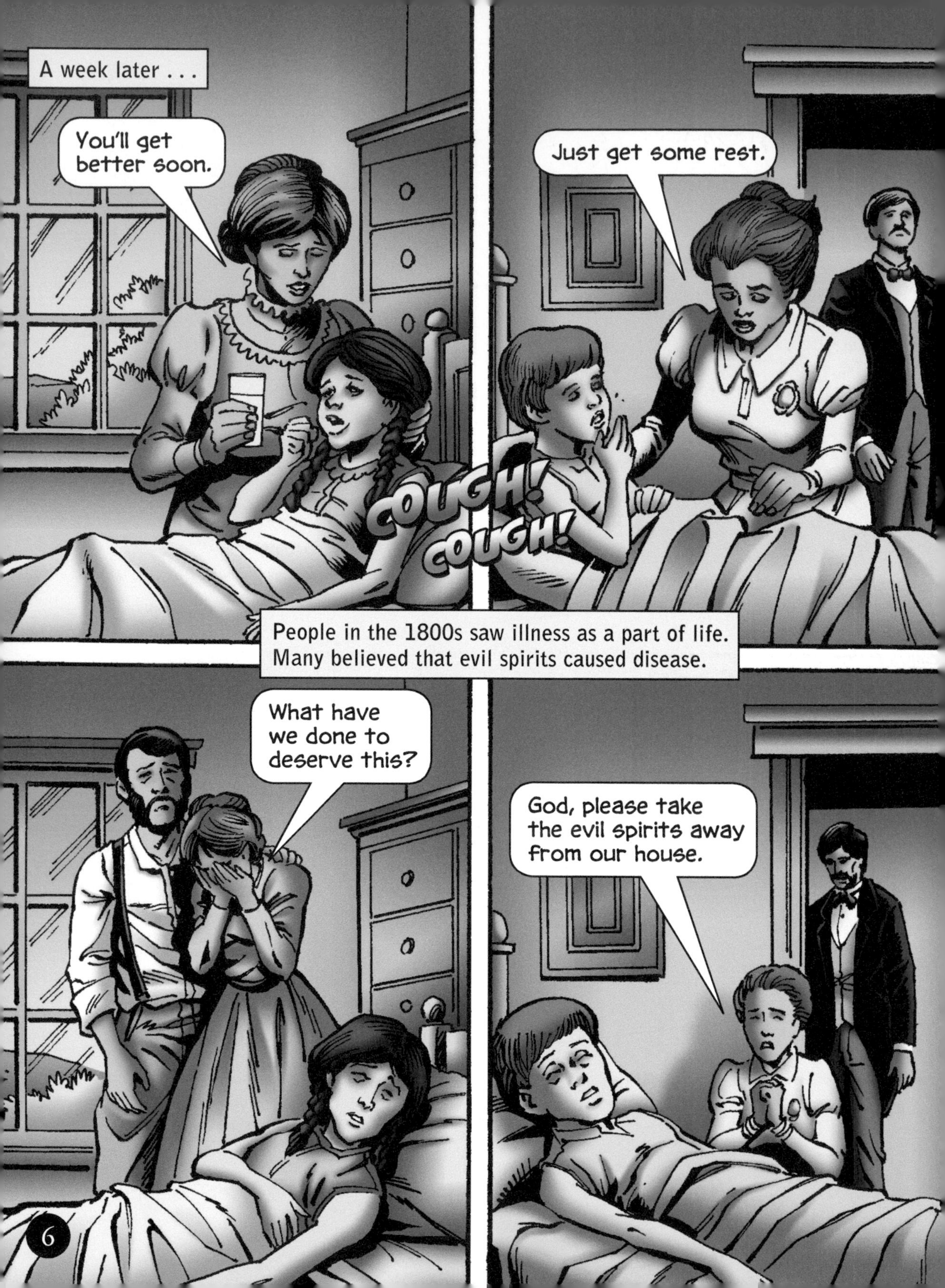

A week later . . .
You'll get better soon.
Just get some rest.
COUGH! COUGH!
People in the 1800s saw illness as a part of life. Many believed that evil spirits caused disease.
What have we done to deserve this?
God, please take the evil spirits away from our house.

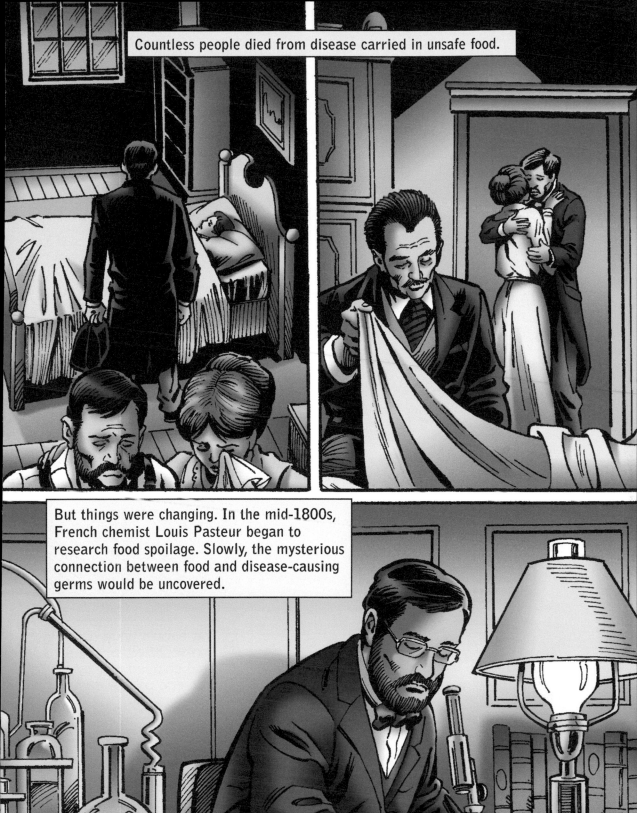

Countless people died from disease carried in unsafe food.

But things were changing. In the mid-1800s, French chemist Louis Pasteur began to research food spoilage. Slowly, the mysterious connection between food and disease-causing germs would be uncovered.

7

Chapter 2
A Living Process

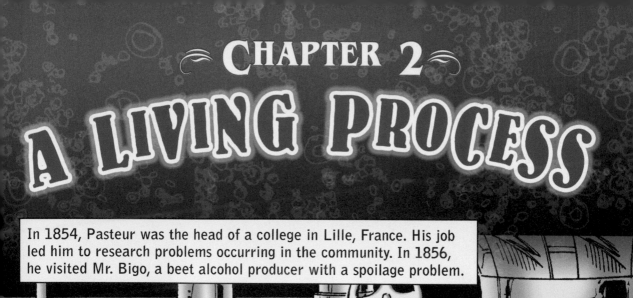

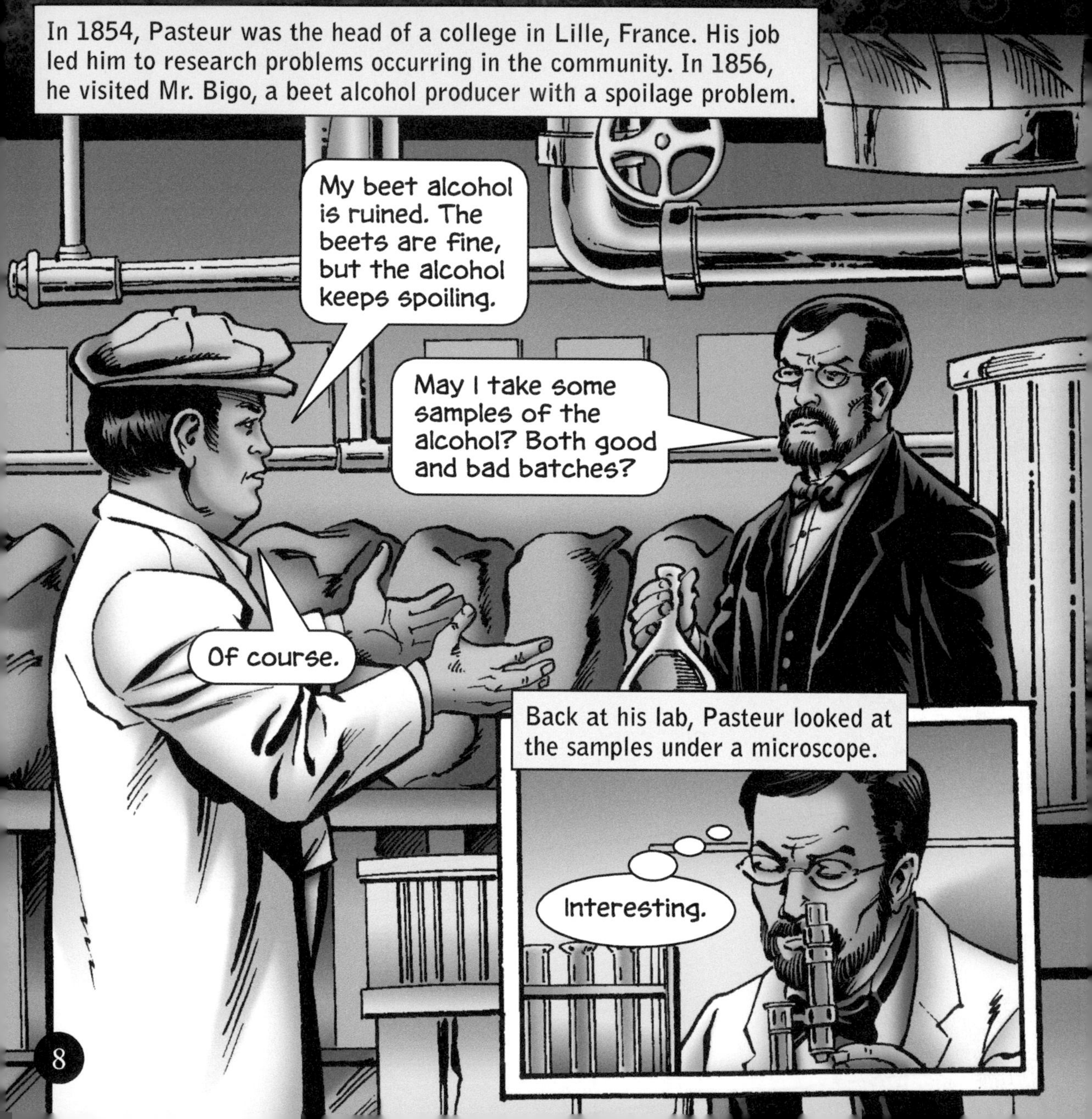
In 1854, Pasteur was the head of a college in Lille, France. His job led him to research problems occurring in the community. In 1856, he visited Mr. Bigo, a beet alcohol producer with a spoilage problem.
My beet alcohol is ruined. The beets are fine, but the alcohol keeps spoiling.
May I take some samples of the alcohol? Both good and bad batches?
Of course.
Back at his lab, Pasteur looked at the samples under a microscope.
Interesting.

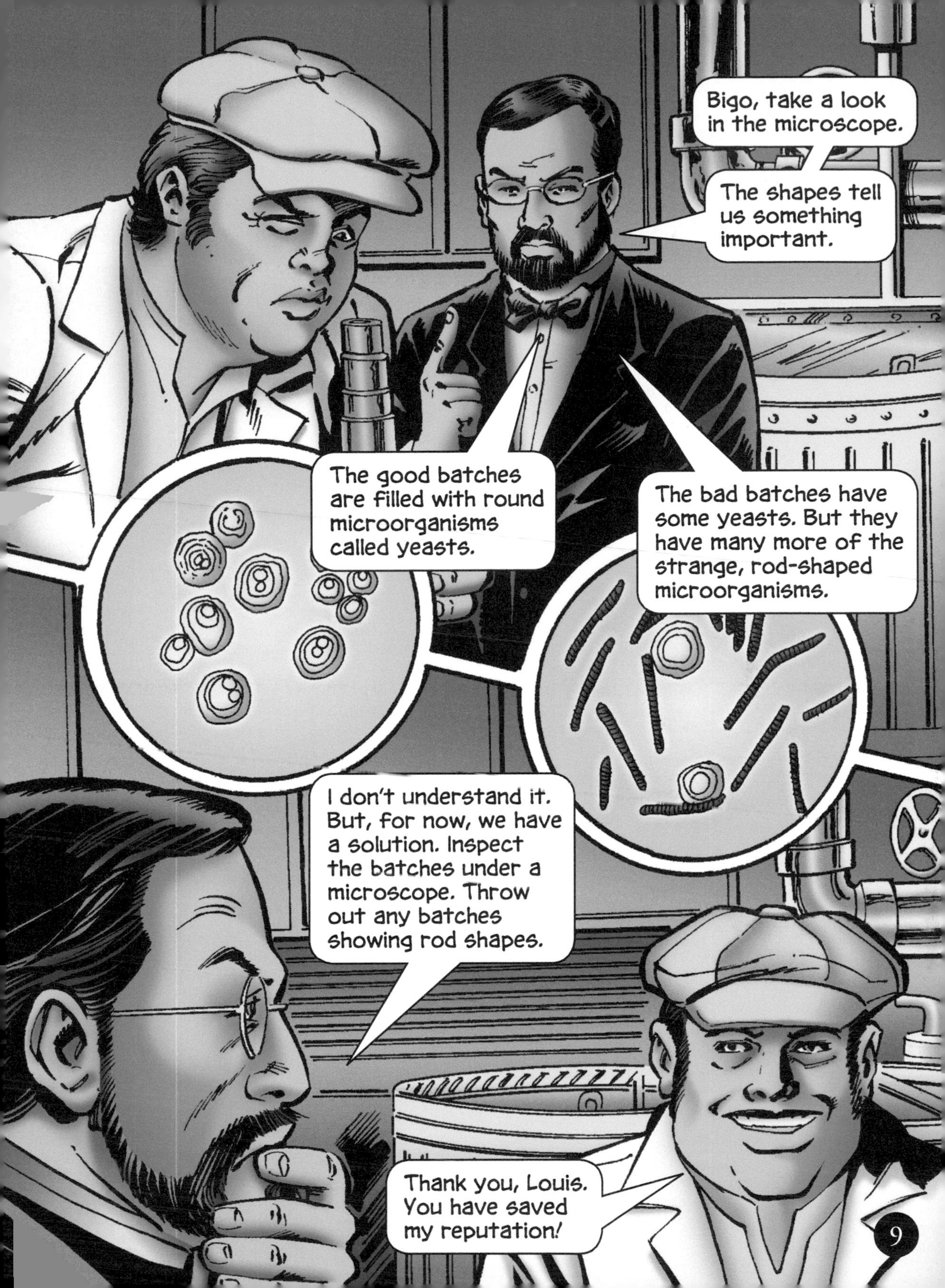

Bigo, take a look in the microscope.
The shapes tell us something important.
The good batches are filled with round microorganisms called yeasts.
The bad batches have some yeasts. But they have many more of the strange, rod-shaped microorganisms.
I don't understand it. But, for now, we have a solution. Inspect the batches under a microscope. Throw out any batches showing rod shapes.
Thank you, Louis. You have saved my reputation!

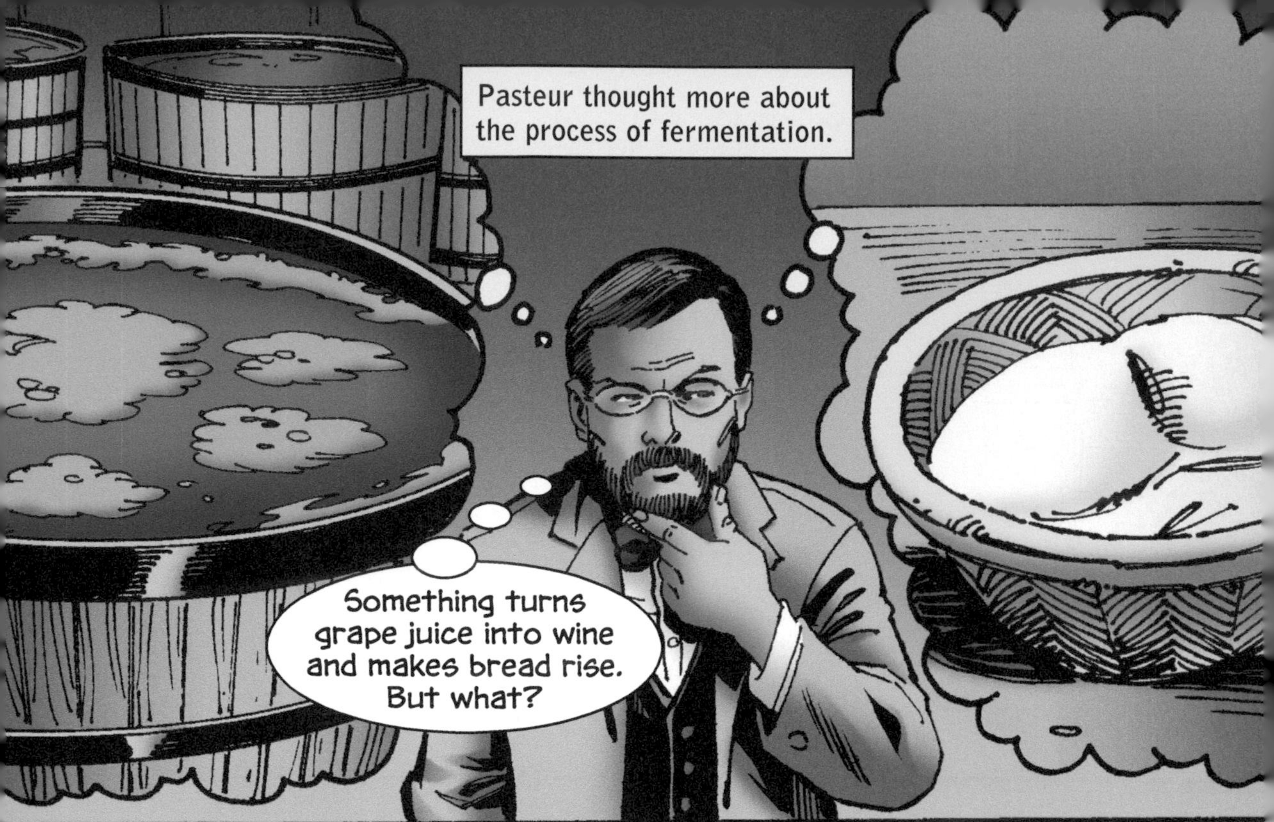
Pasteur thought more about the process of fermentation.
Something turns grape juice into wine and makes bread rise. But what?

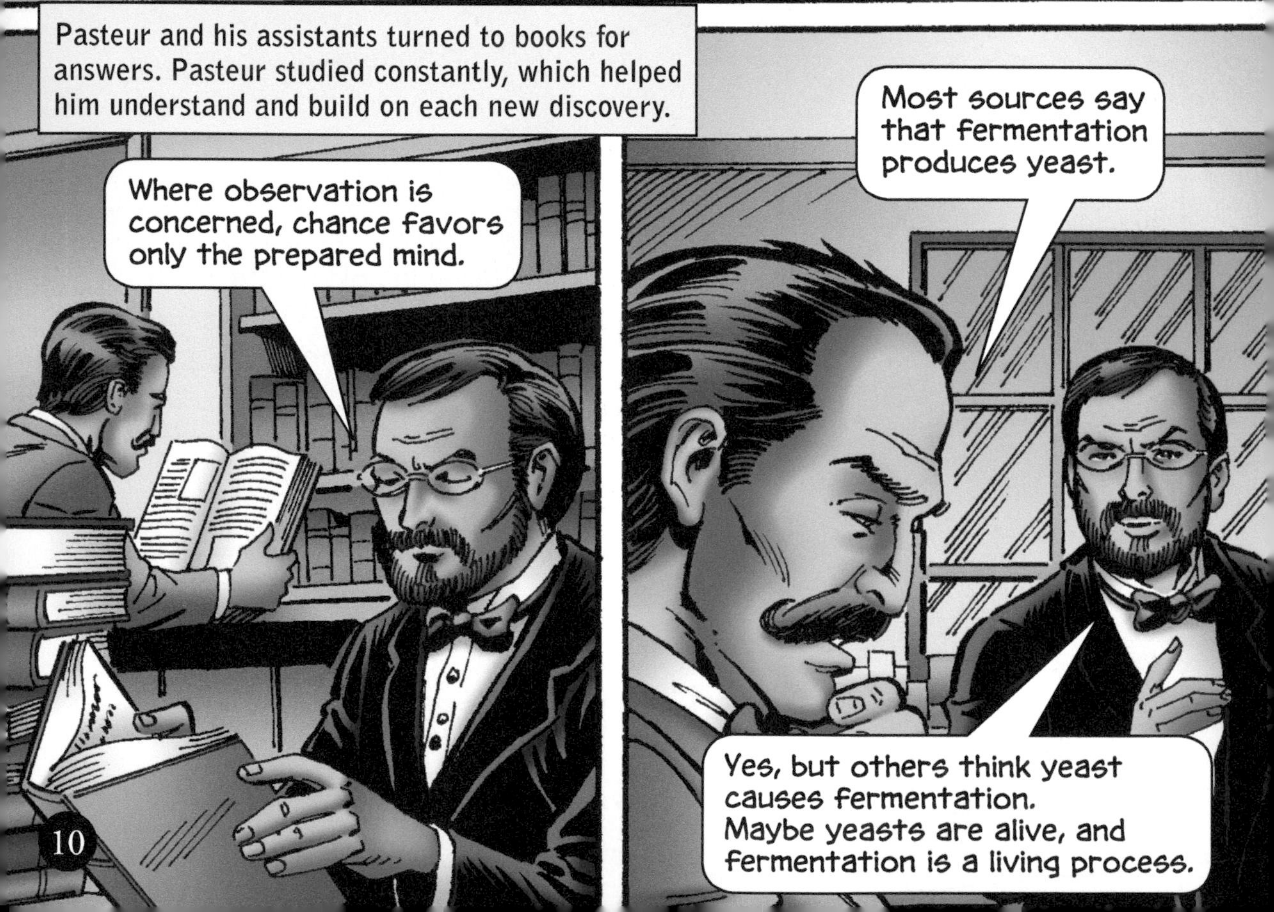
Pasteur and his assistants turned to books for answers. Pasteur studied constantly, which helped him understand and build on each new discovery.
Where observation is concerned, chance favors only the prepared mind.
Most sources say that fermentation produces yeast.
Yes, but others think yeast causes fermentation.
Maybe yeasts are alive, and fermentation is a living process.

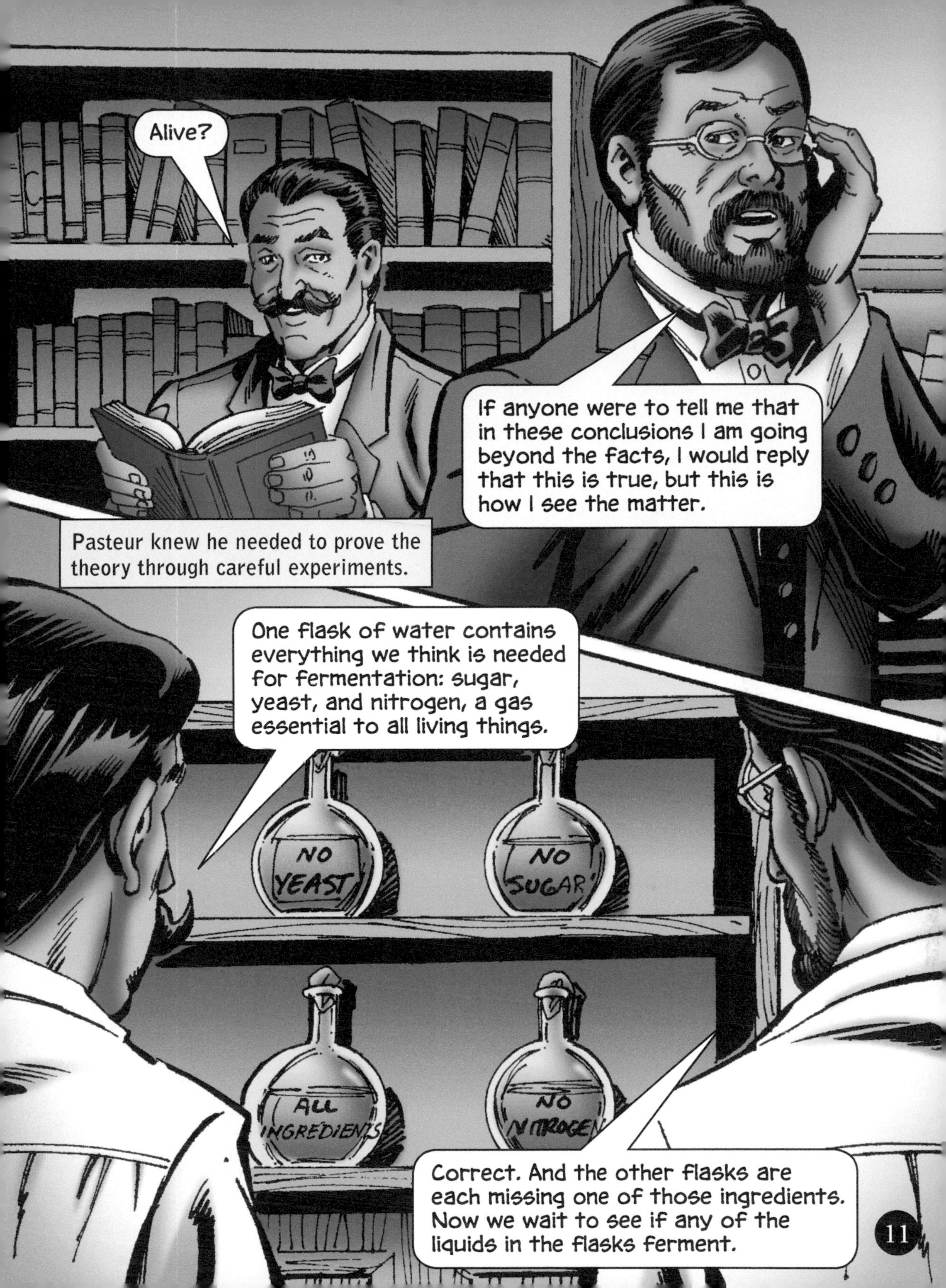

Alive?
If anyone were to tell me that in these conclusions I am going beyond the facts, I would reply that this is true, but this is how I see the matter.
Pasteur knew he needed to prove the theory through careful experiments.
One flask of water contains everything we think is needed for fermentation: sugar, yeast, and nitrogen, a gas essential to all living things.
NO YEAST
NO SUGAR
ALL INGREDIENTS
NO NITROGEN
Correct. And the other flasks are each missing one of those ingredients. Now we wait to see if any of the liquids in the flasks ferment.

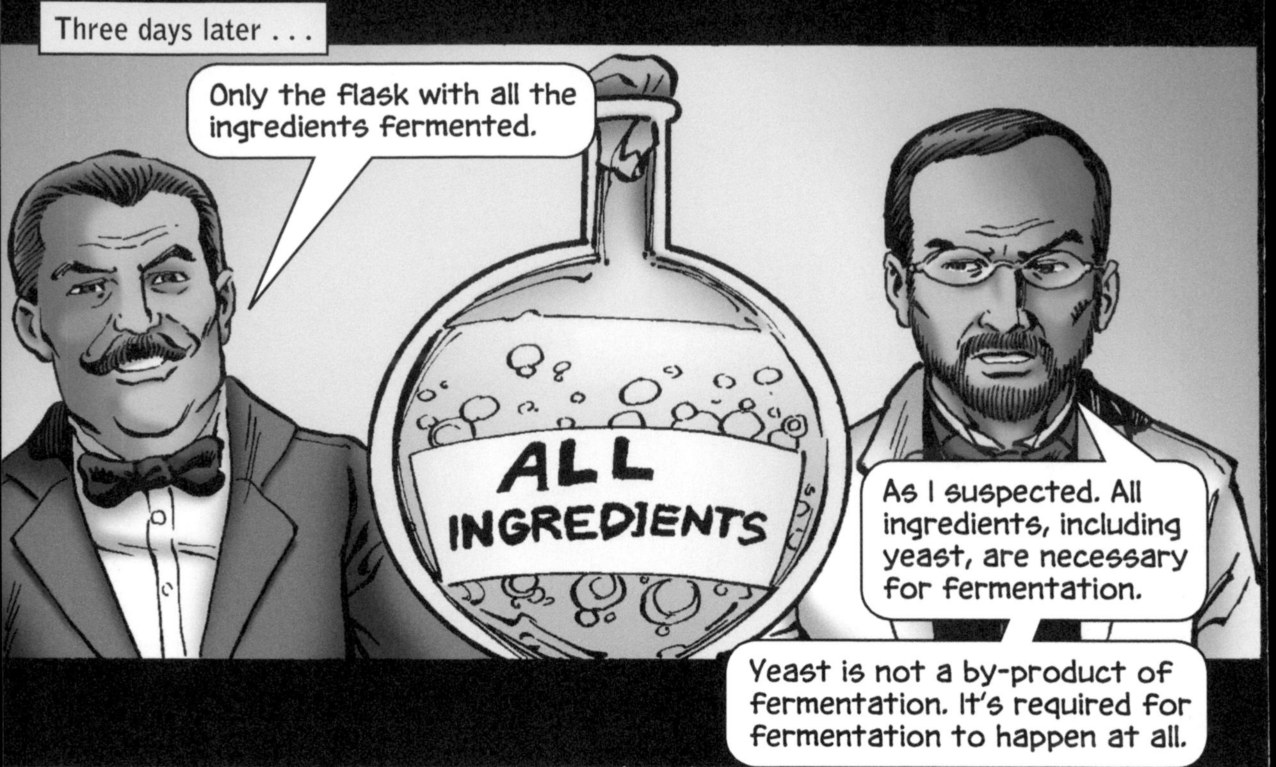
Three days later . . .
Only the flask with all the ingredients fermented.
ALL INGREDIENTS
As I suspected. All ingredients, including yeast, are necessary for fermentation.
Yeast is not a by-product of fermentation. It's required for fermentation to happen at all.

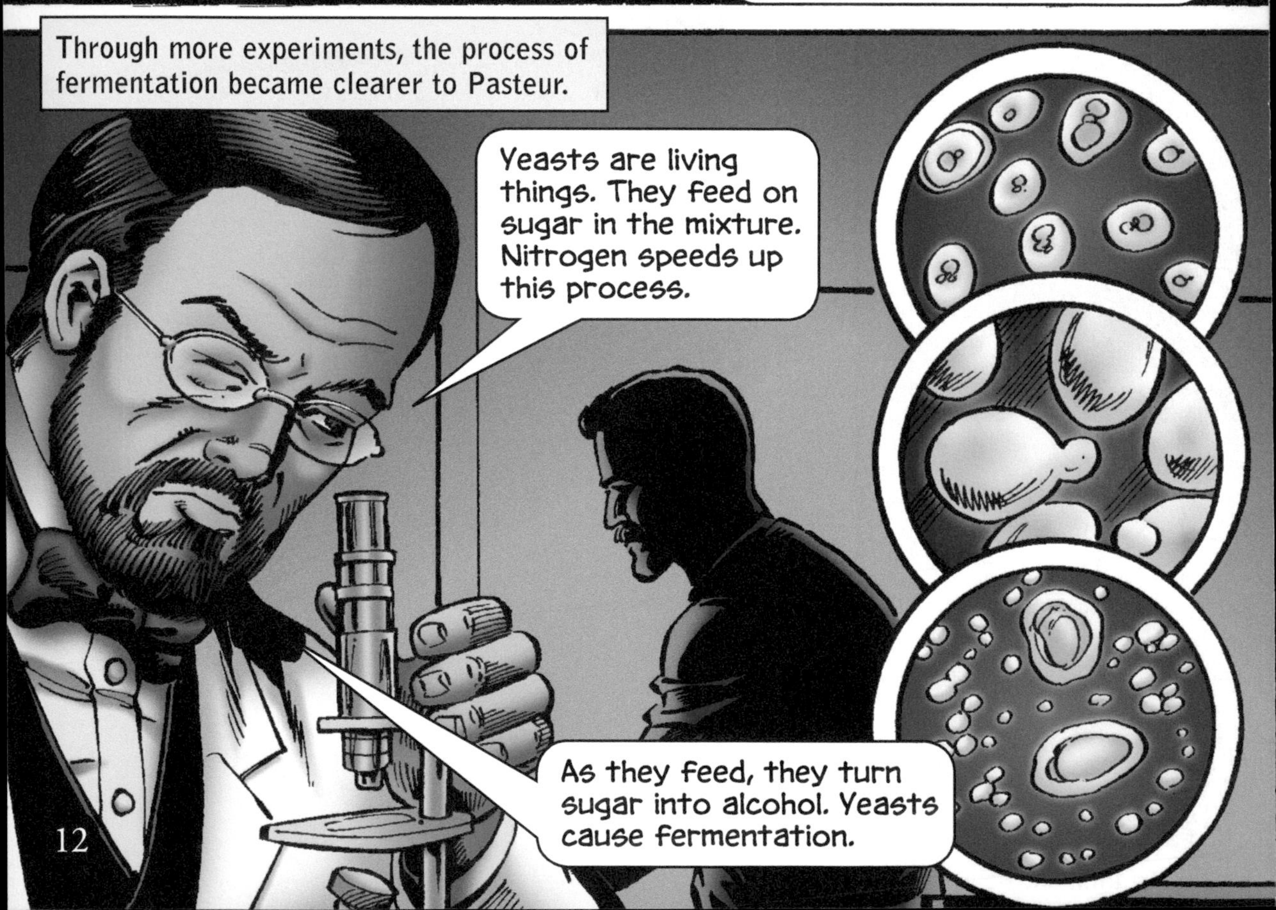
Through more experiments, the process of fermentation became clearer to Pasteur.
Yeasts are living things. They feed on sugar in the mixture. Nitrogen speeds up this process.
As they feed, they turn sugar into alcohol. Yeasts cause fermentation.

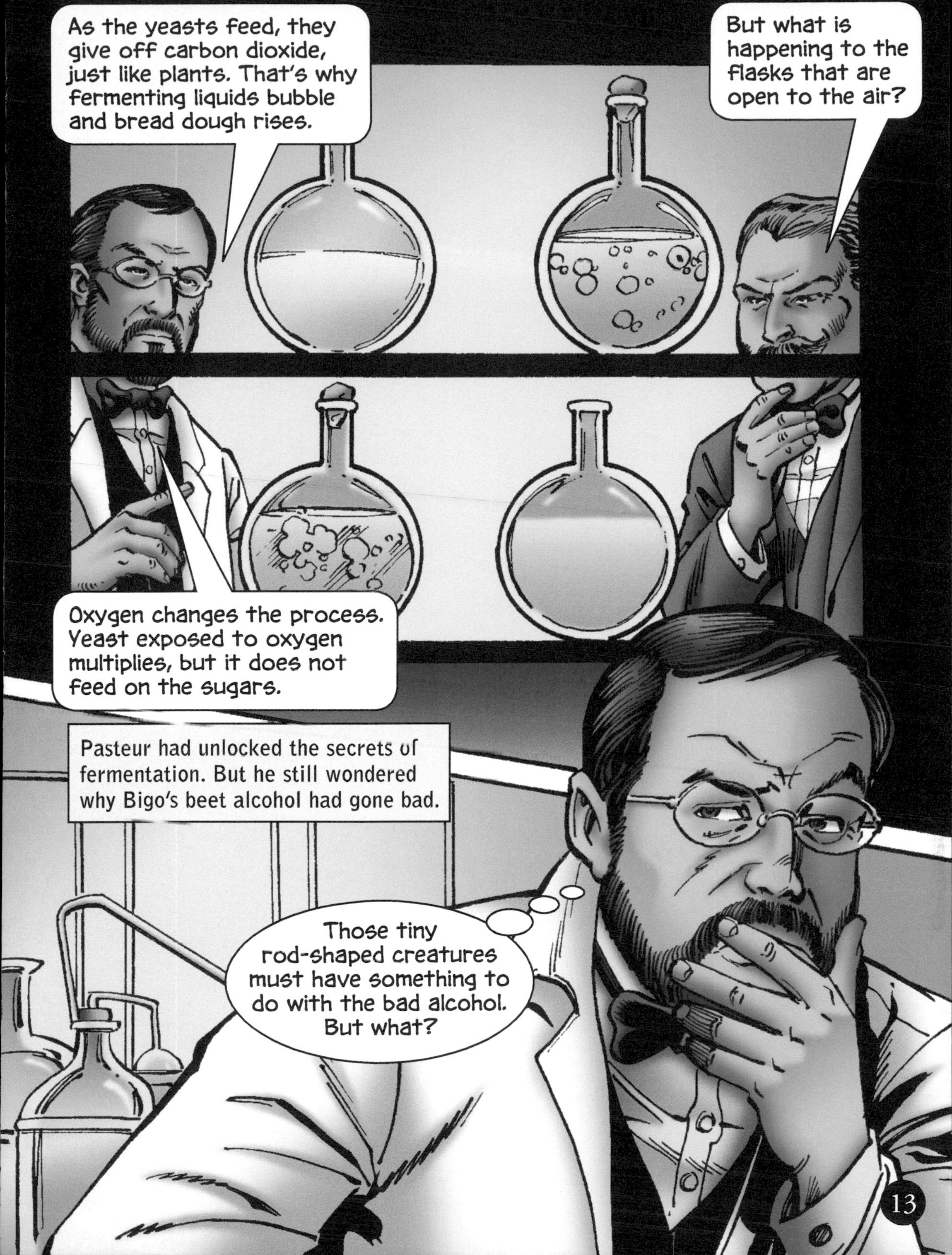
As the yeasts feed, they give off carbon dioxide, just like plants. That's why fermenting liquids bubble and bread dough rises.
But what is happening to the flasks that are open to the air?
Oxygen changes the process. Yeast exposed to oxygen multiplies, but it does not feed on the sugars.
Pasteur had unlocked the secrets of fermentation. But he still wondered why Bigo's beet alcohol had gone bad.
Those tiny rod-shaped creatures must have something to do with the bad alcohol. But what?

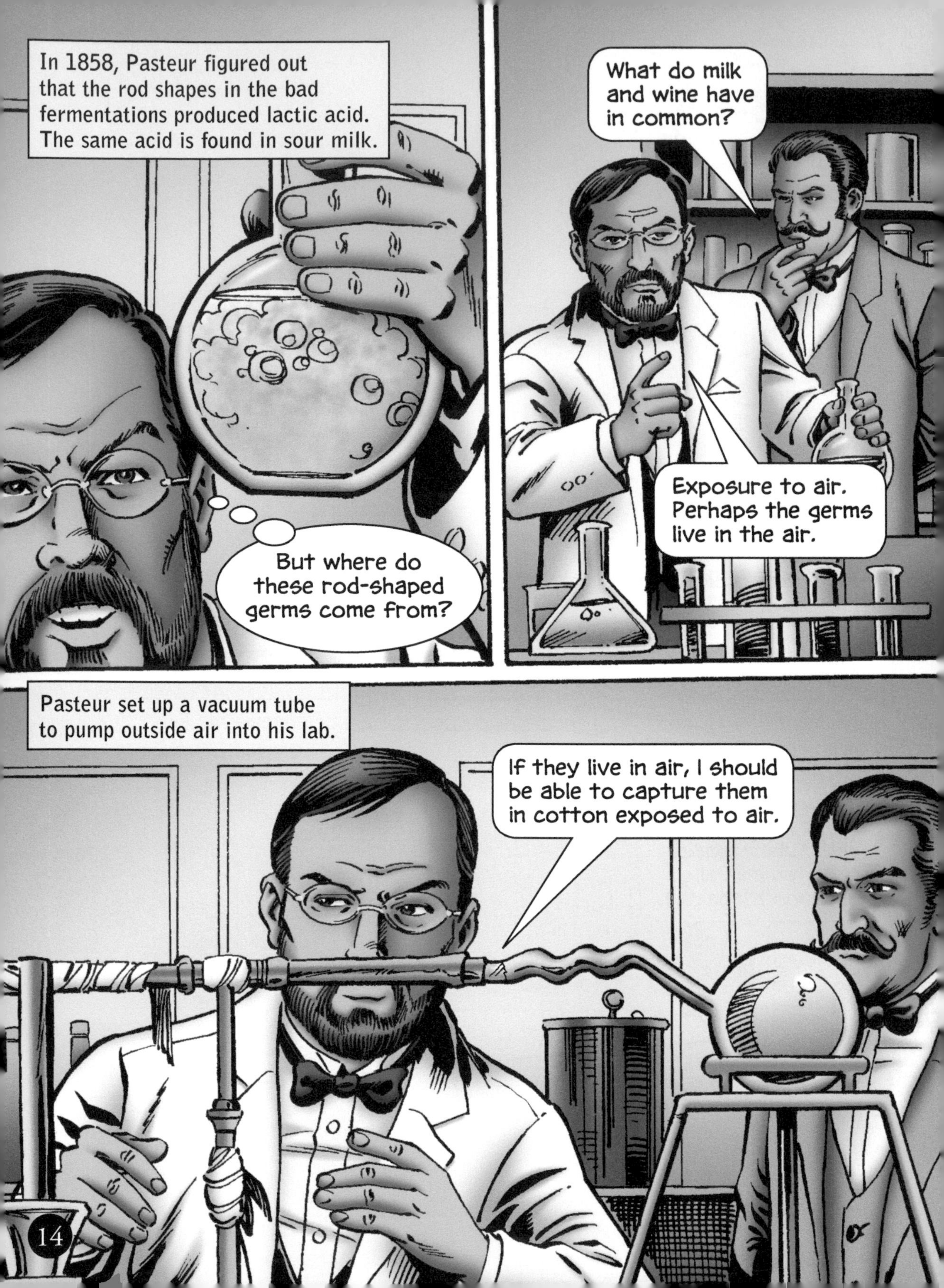
In 1858, Pasteur figured out that the rod shapes in the bad fermentations produced lactic acid. The same acid is found in sour milk.
But where do these rod-shaped germs come from?
What do milk and wine have in common?
Exposure to air. Perhaps the germs live in the air.
Pasteur set up a vacuum tube to pump outside air into his lab.
If they live in air, I should be able to capture them in cotton exposed to air.

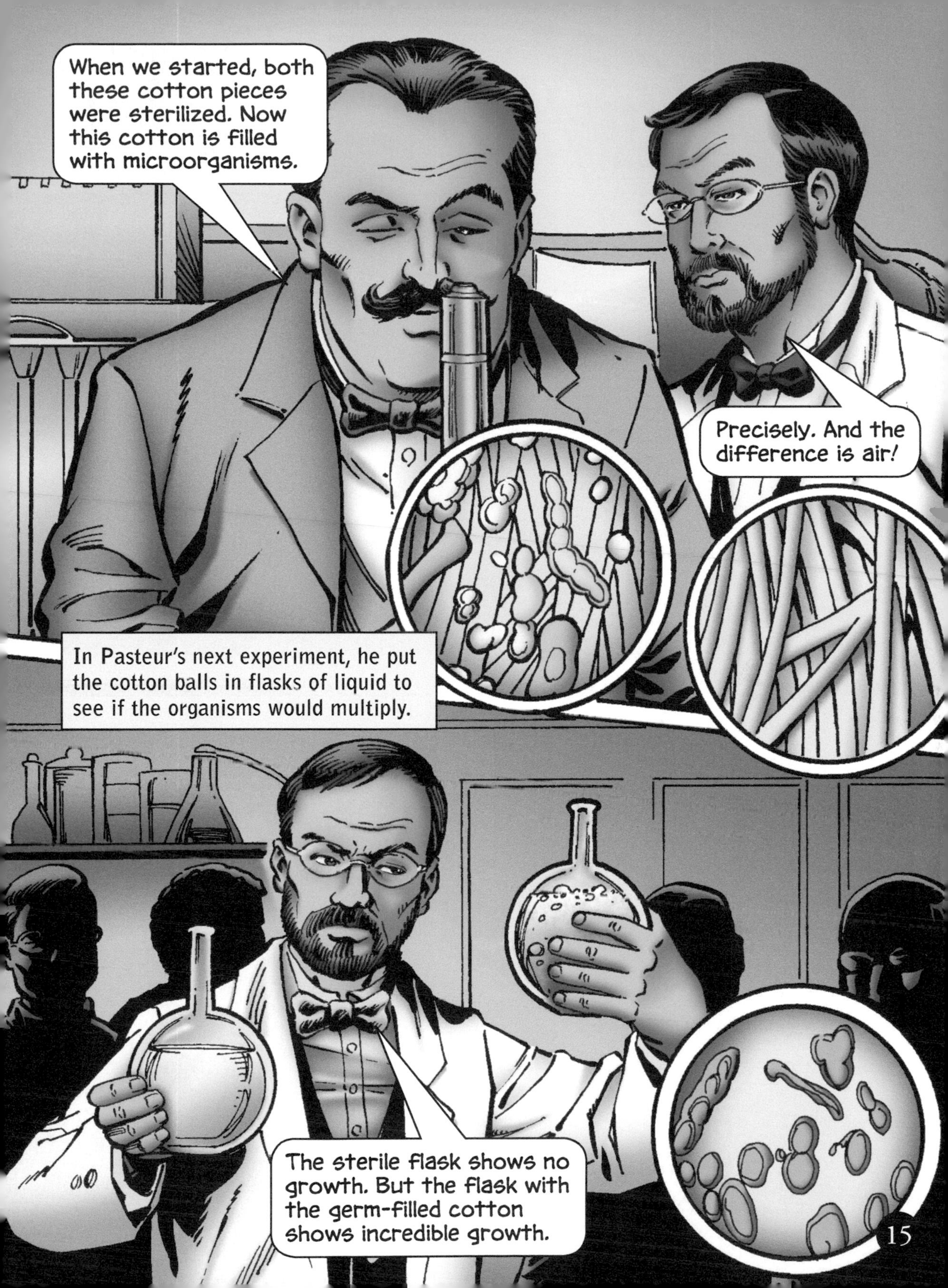
When we started, both these cotton pieces were sterilized. Now this cotton is filled with microorganisms.
Precisely. And the difference is air!
In Pasteur's next experiment, he put the cotton balls in flasks of liquid to see if the organisms would multiply.
The sterile flask shows no growth. But the flask with the germ-filled cotton shows incredible growth.

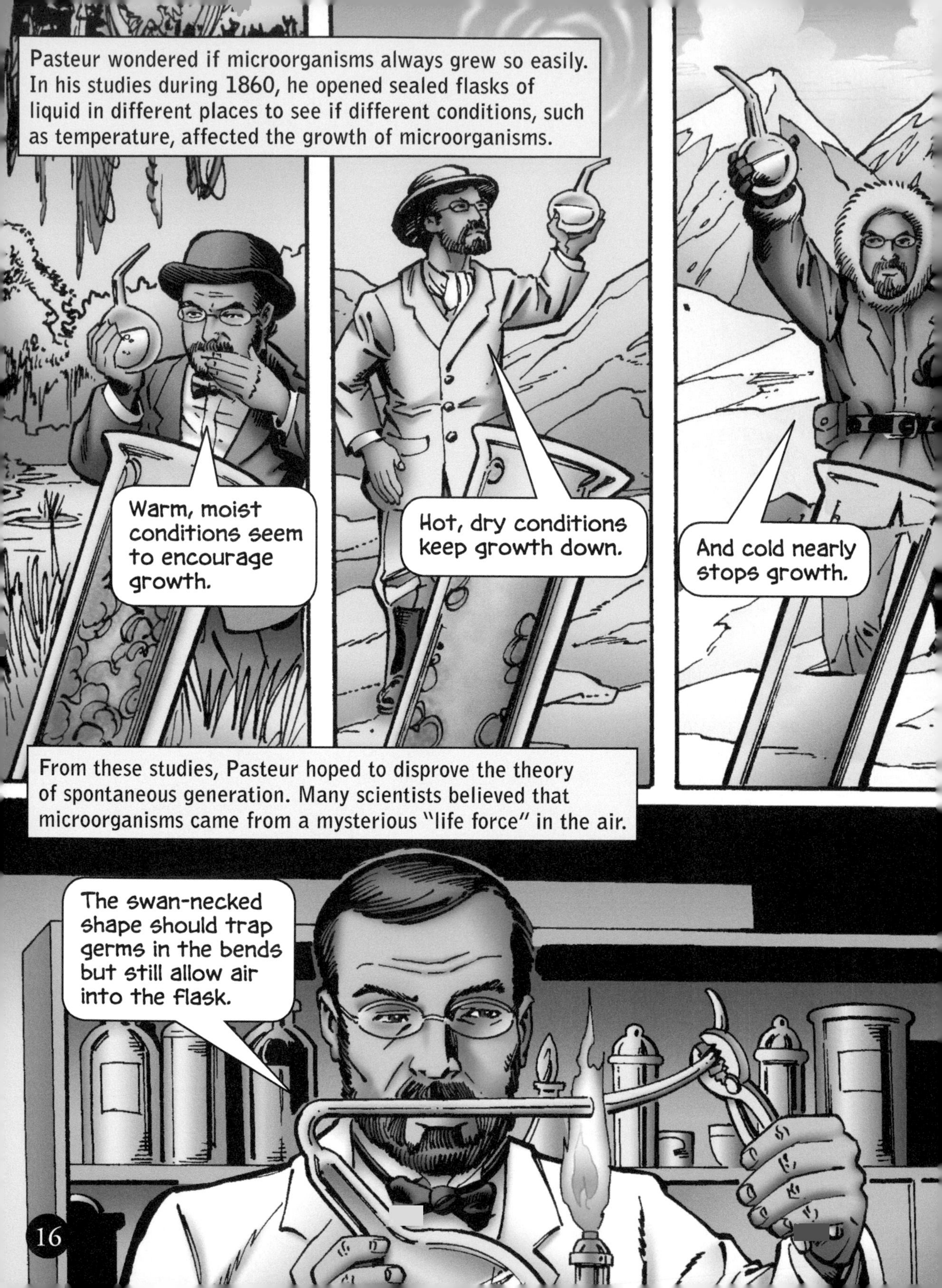
Pasteur wondered if microorganisms always grew so easily. In his studies during 1860, he opened sealed flasks of liquid in different places to see if different conditions, such as temperature, affected the growth of microorganisms.
Warm, moist conditions seem to encourage growth.
Hot, dry conditions keep growth down.
And cold nearly stops growth.
From these studies, Pasteur hoped to disprove the theory of spontaneous generation. Many scientists believed that microorganisms came from a mysterious "life force" in the air.
The swan-necked shape should trap germs in the bends but still allow air into the flask.

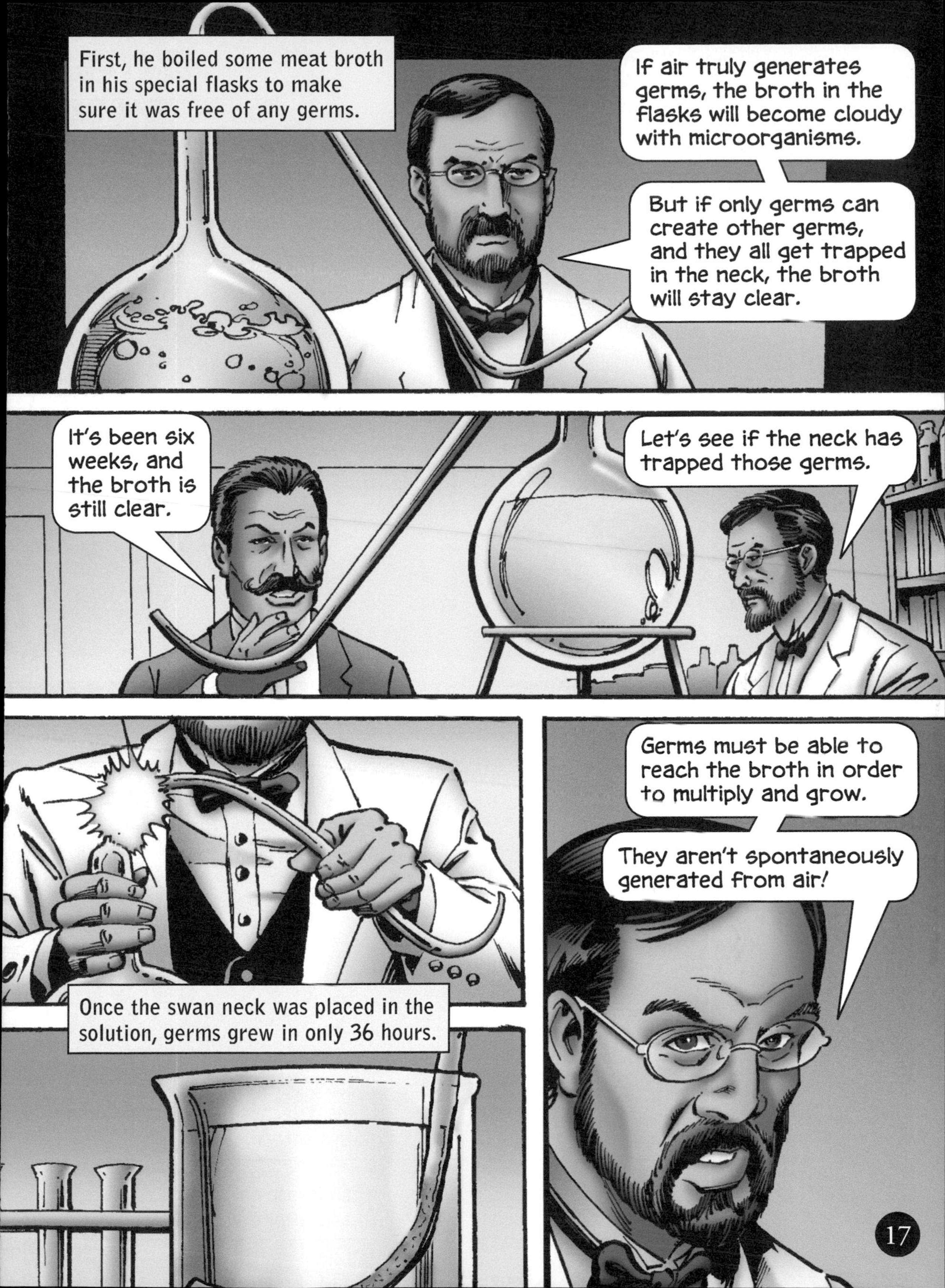
First, he boiled some meat broth in his special flasks to make sure it was free of any germs.
If air truly generates germs, the broth in the flasks will become cloudy with microorganisms.
But if only germs can create other germs, and they all get trapped in the neck, the broth will stay clear.
It's been six weeks, and the broth is still clear.
Let's see if the neck has trapped those germs.
Once the swan neck was placed in the solution, germs grew in only 36 hours.
Germs must be able to reach the broth in order to multiply and grow.
They aren't spontaneously generated from air!

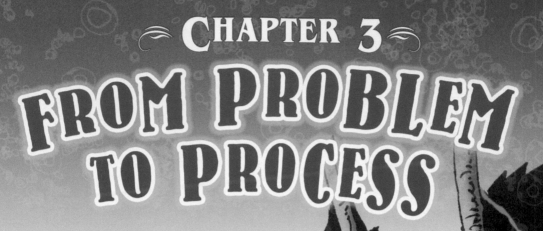

CHAPTER 3
FROM PROBLEM TO PROCESS

In 1861, Pasteur won the Zecker Prize from the Academy of Sciences in Paris for disproving spontaneous generation. After winning the award, Pasteur was asked by France's king, Napoleon III, to help France's wine industry. France exported a lot of wine to other countries, but it often arrived spoiled.

Are there any problems with your grapes?

No. They look and taste like they always do.

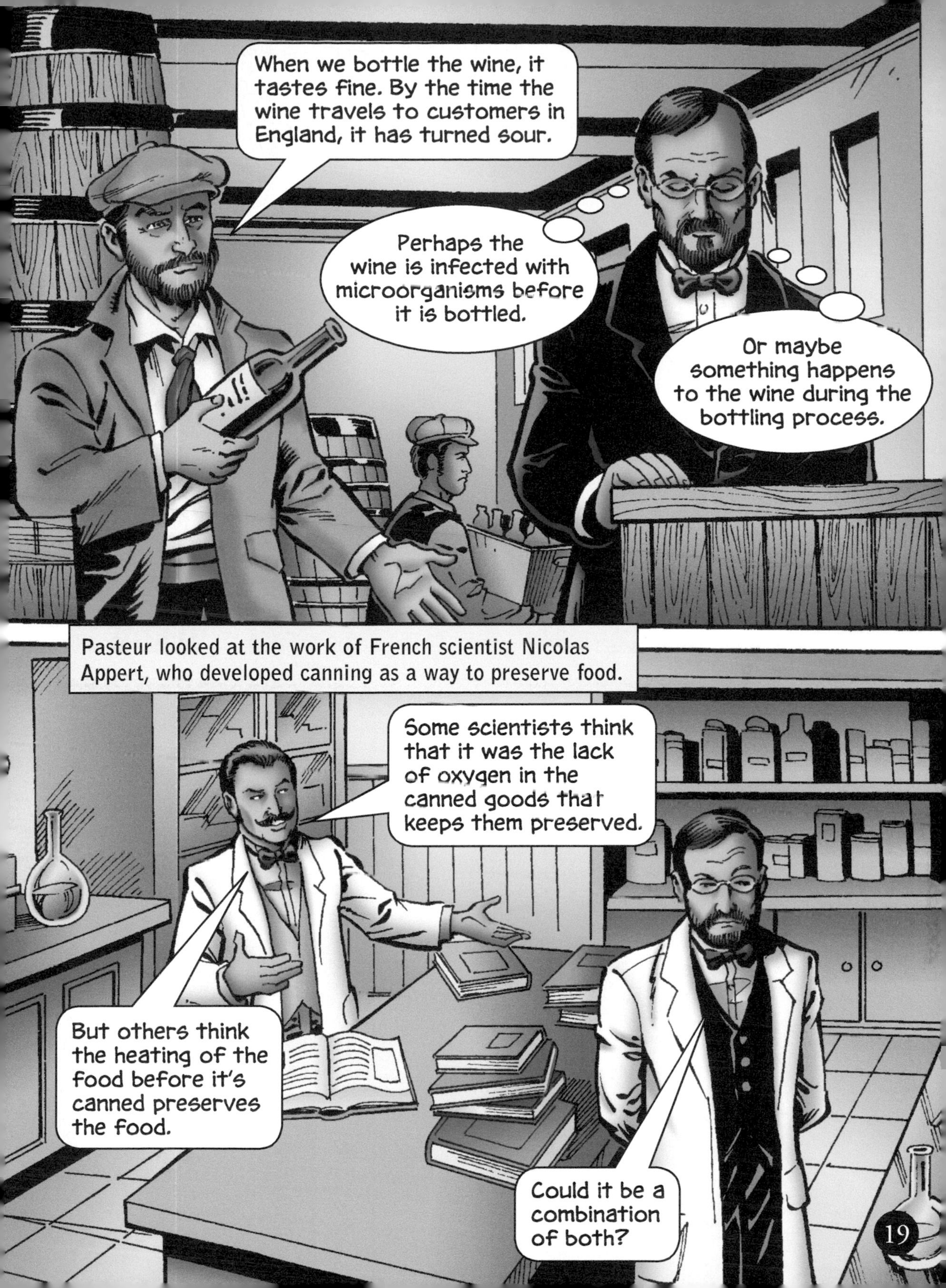
When we bottle the wine, it tastes fine. By the time the wine travels to customers in England, it has turned sour.
Perhaps the wine is infected with microorganisms before it is bottled.
Or maybe something happens to the wine during the bottling process.
Pasteur looked at the work of French scientist Nicolas Appert, who developed canning as a way to preserve food.
Some scientists think that it was the lack of oxygen in the canned goods that keeps them preserved.
But others think the heating of the food before it's canned preserves the food.
Could it be a combination of both?

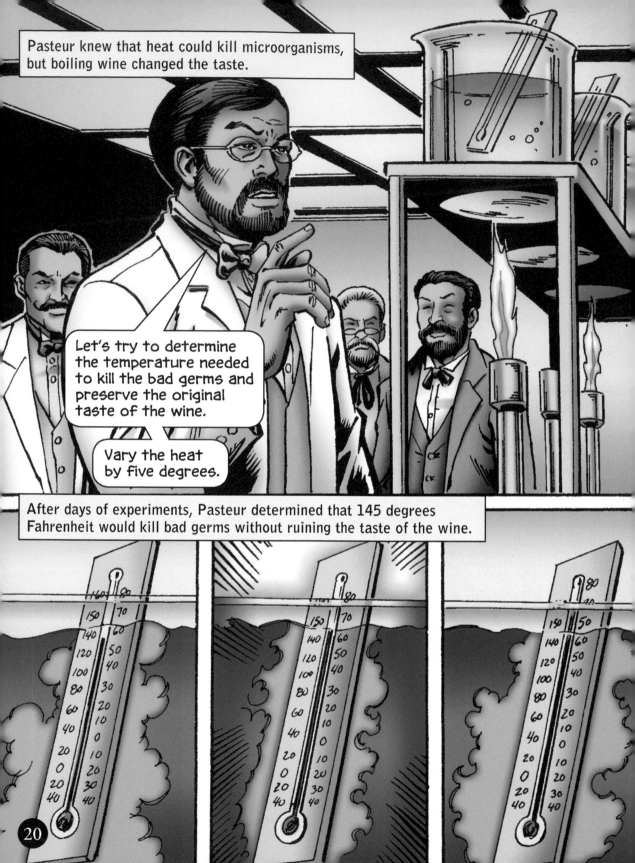

Pasteur knew that heat could kill microorganisms, but boiling wine changed the taste.

Let's try to determine the temperature needed to kill the bad germs and preserve the original taste of the wine.

Vary the heat by five degrees.

After days of experiments, Pasteur determined that 145 degrees Fahrenheit would kill bad germs without ruining the taste of the wine.

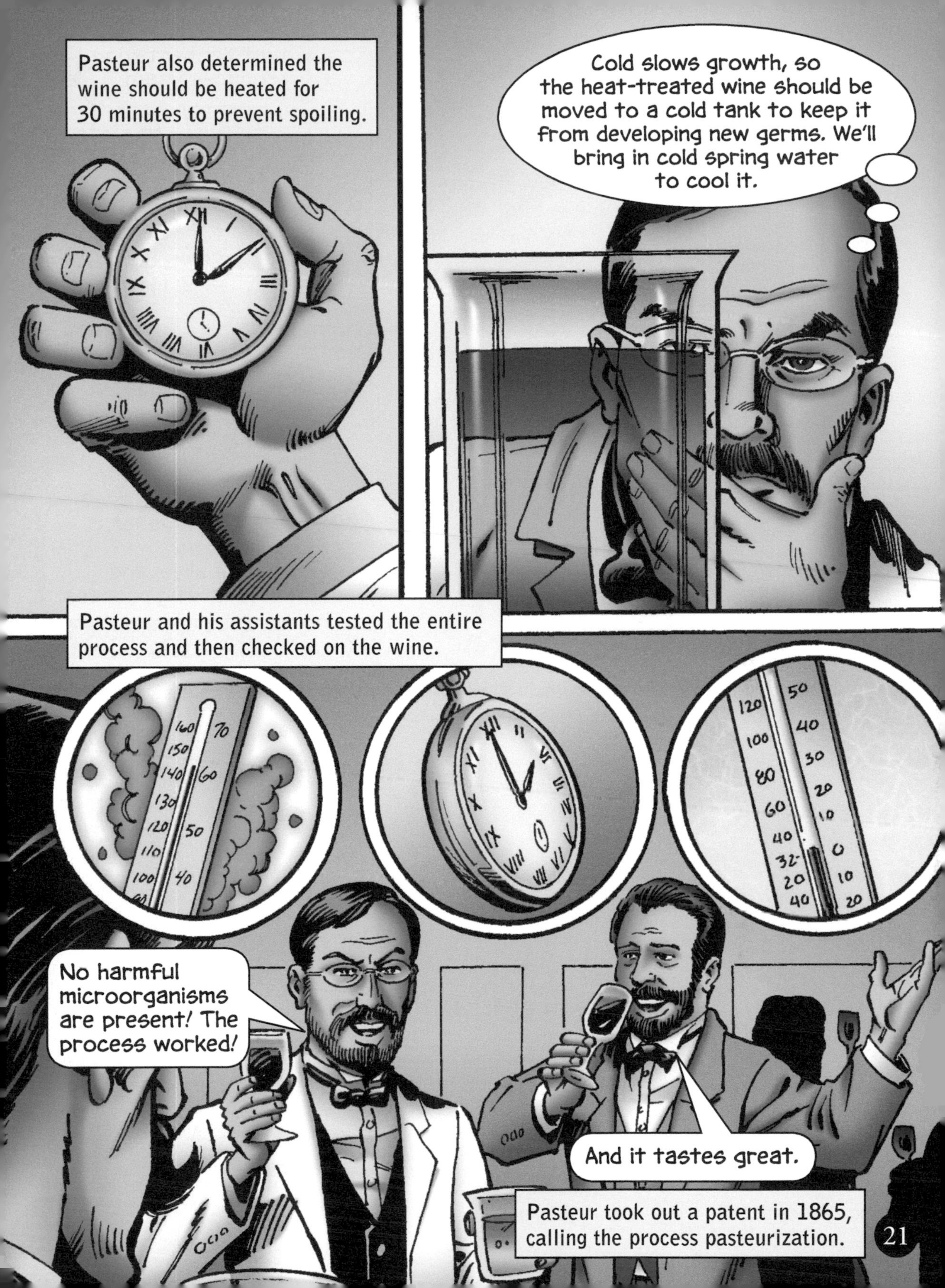
Pasteur also determined the wine should be heated for 30 minutes to prevent spoiling.
Cold slows growth, so the heat-treated wine should be moved to a cold tank to keep it from developing new germs. We'll bring in cold spring water to cool it.
Pasteur and his assistants tested the entire process and then checked on the wine.
No harmful microorganisms are present! The process worked!
And it tastes great.
Pasteur took out a patent in 1865, calling the process pasteurization.

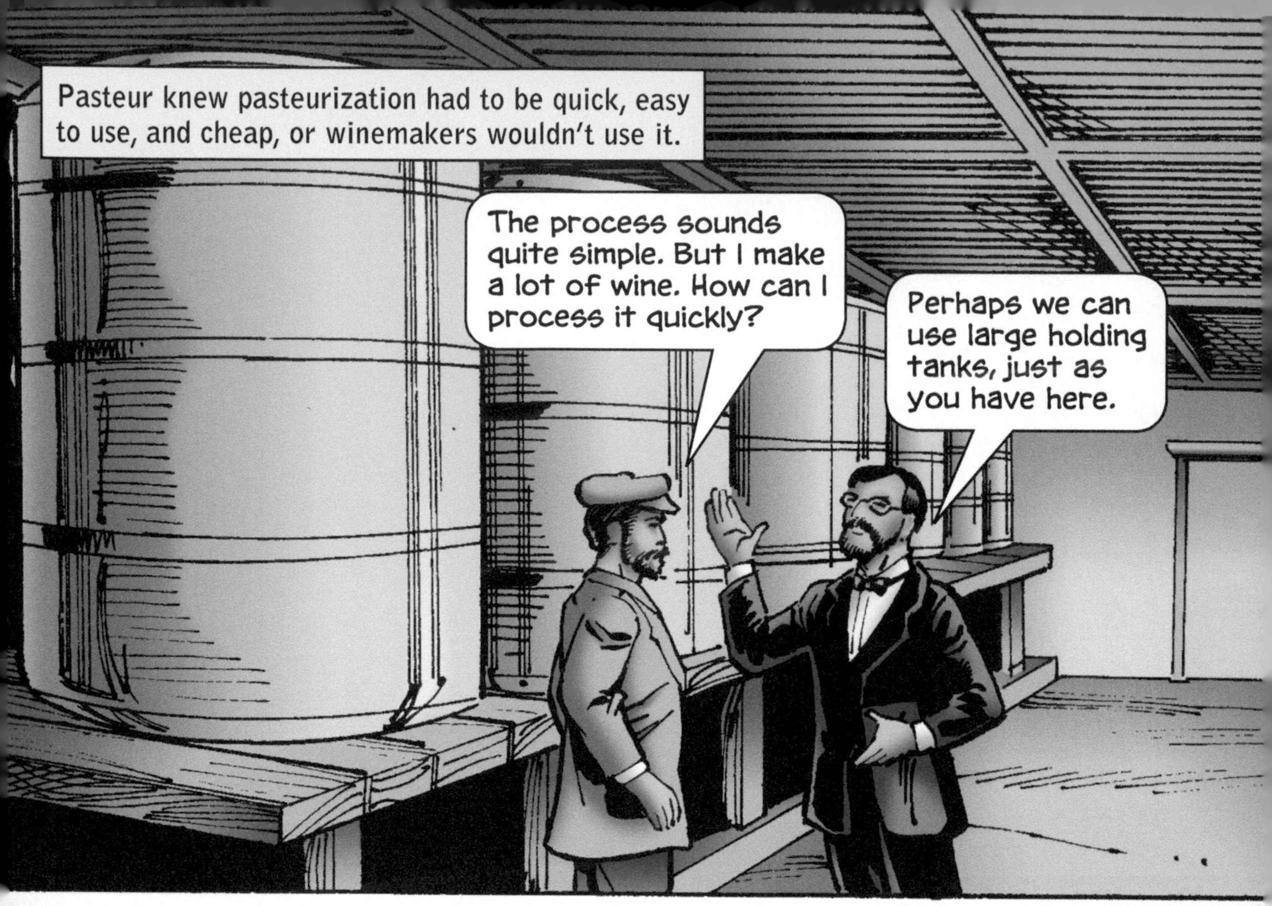
Pasteur knew pasteurization had to be quick, easy to use, and cheap, or winemakers wouldn't use it.
The process sounds quite simple. But I make a lot of wine. How can I process it quickly?
Perhaps we can use large holding tanks, just as you have here.

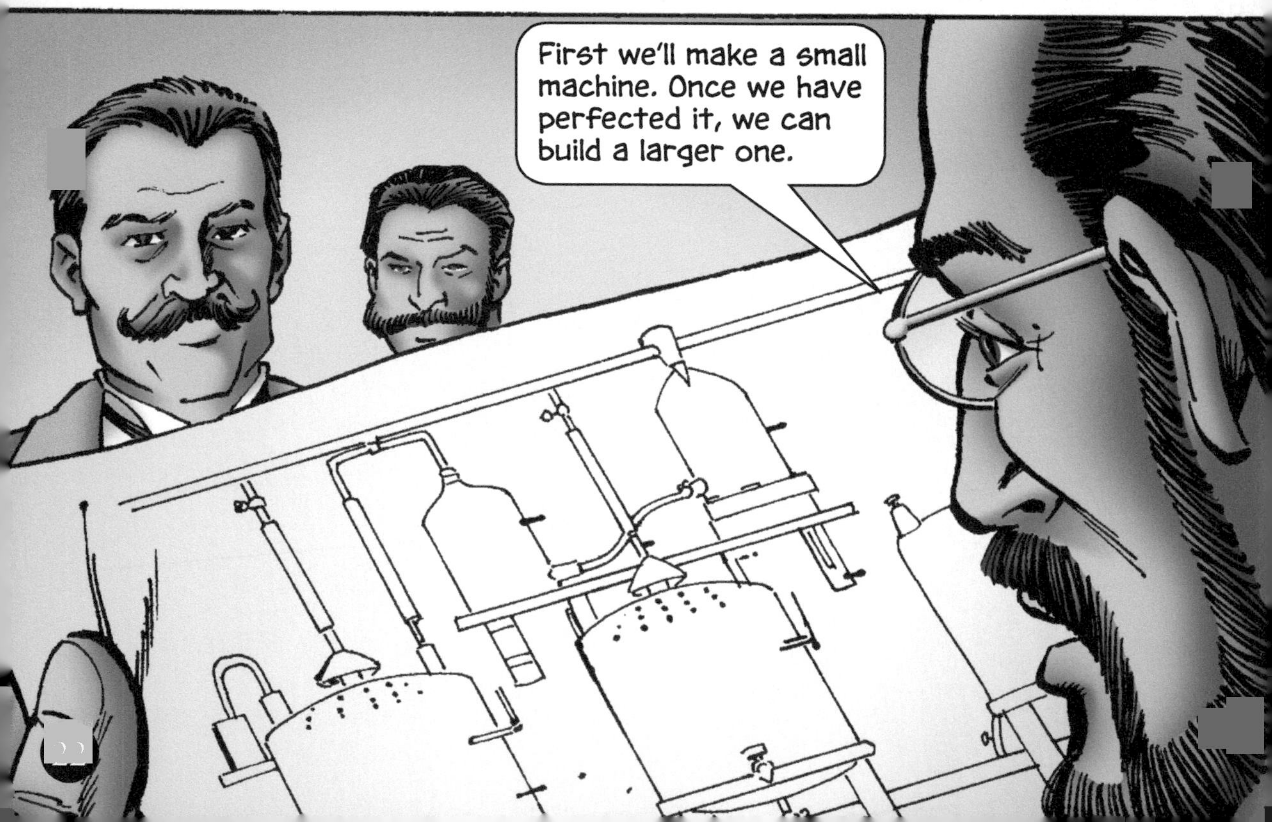
First we'll make a small machine. Once we have perfected it, we can build a larger one.

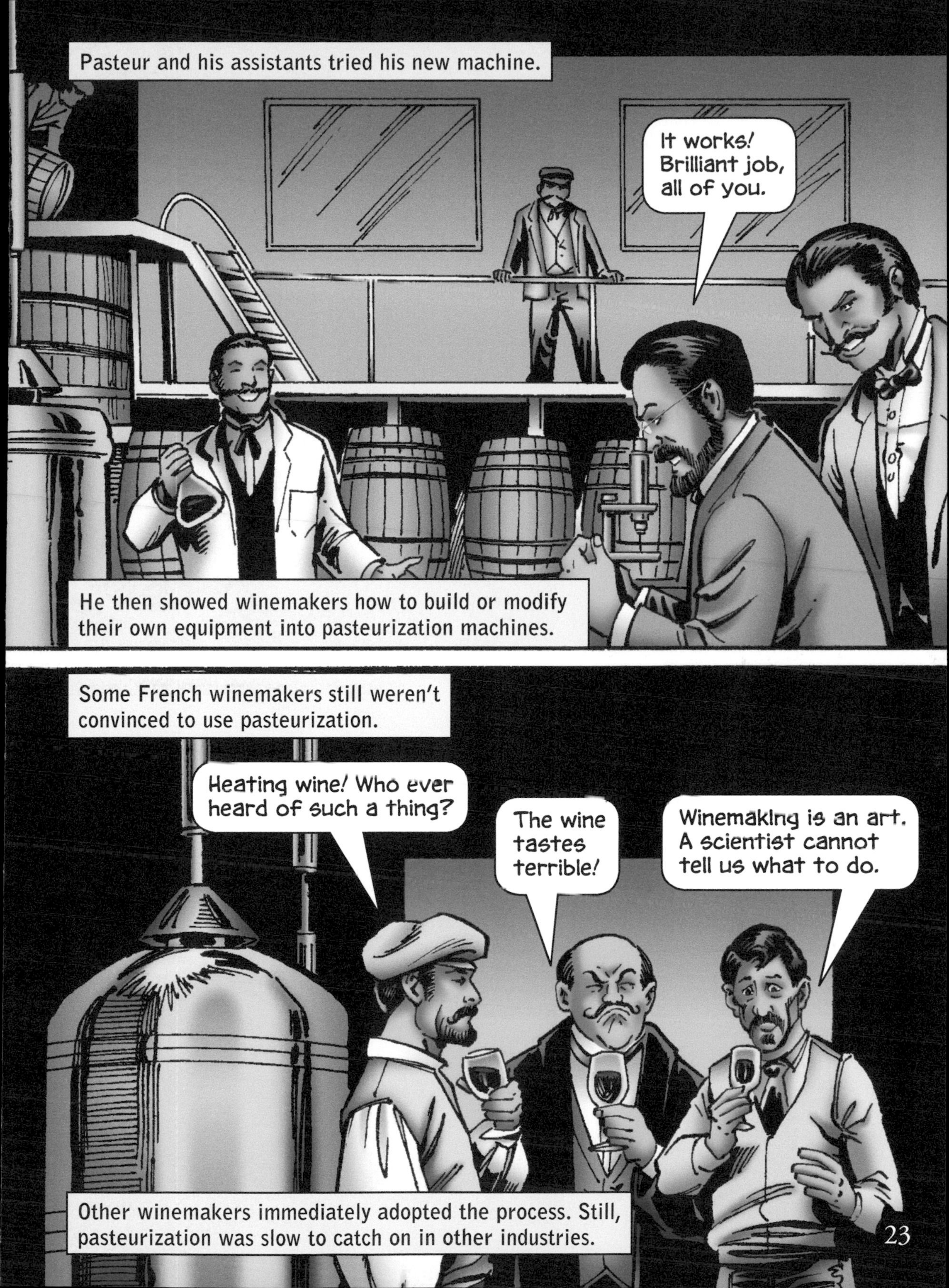
Pasteur and his assistants tried his new machine.
It works! Brilliant job, all of you.
He then showed winemakers how to build or modify their own equipment into pasteurization machines.
Some French winemakers still weren't convinced to use pasteurization.
Heating wine! Who ever heard of such a thing?
The wine tastes terrible!
Winemaking is an art. A scientist cannot tell us what to do.
Other winemakers immediately adopted the process. Still, pasteurization was slow to catch on in other industries.

CHAPTER 4

PASTEURIZATION FOR HEALTH

Louis Pasteur's work with germs made him an early supporter of the germ theory of disease. Soon, new discoveries about germs would give pasteurization a new purpose.

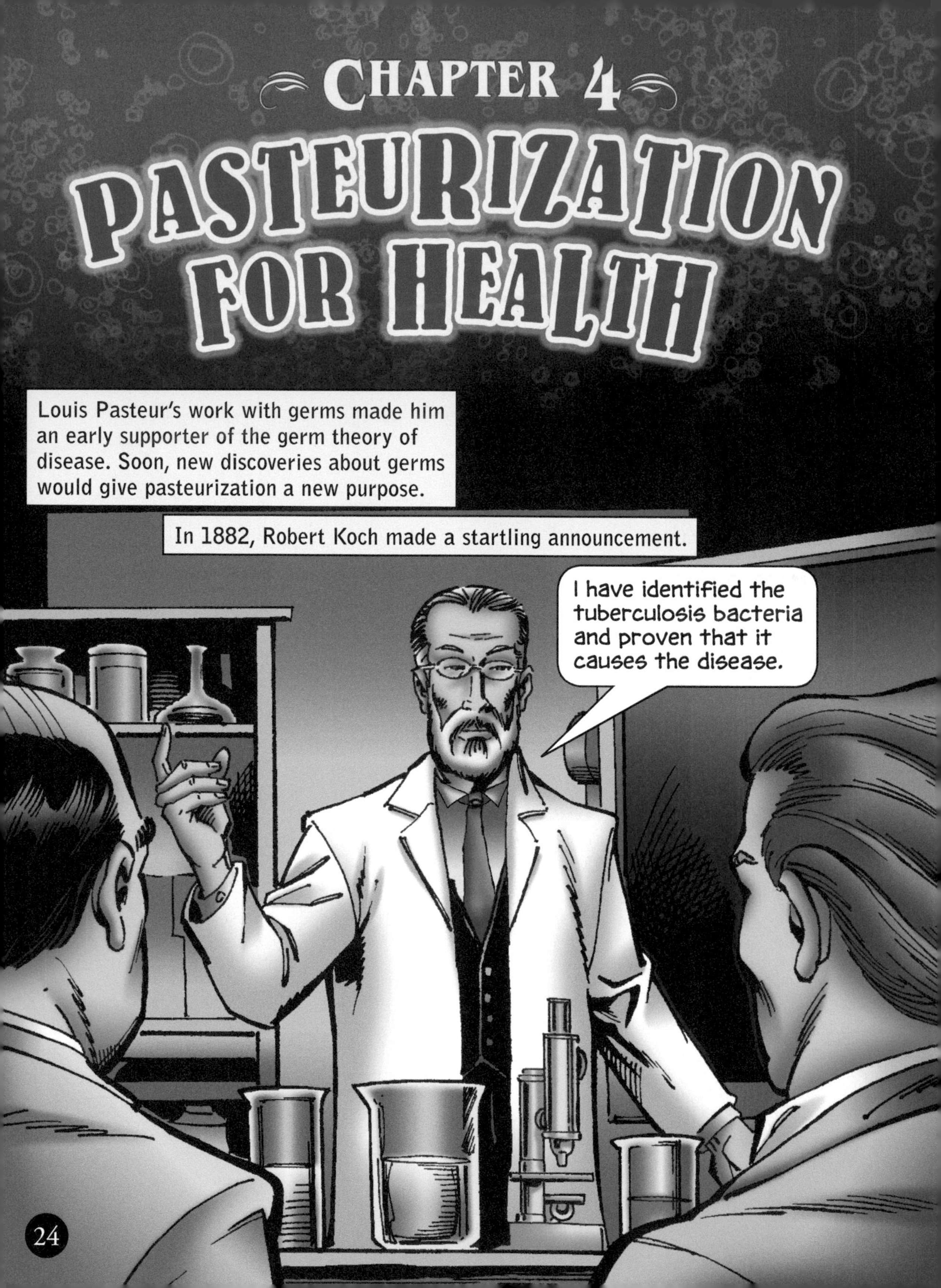
In 1882, Robert Koch made a startling announcement.
I have identified the tuberculosis bacteria and proven that it causes the disease.

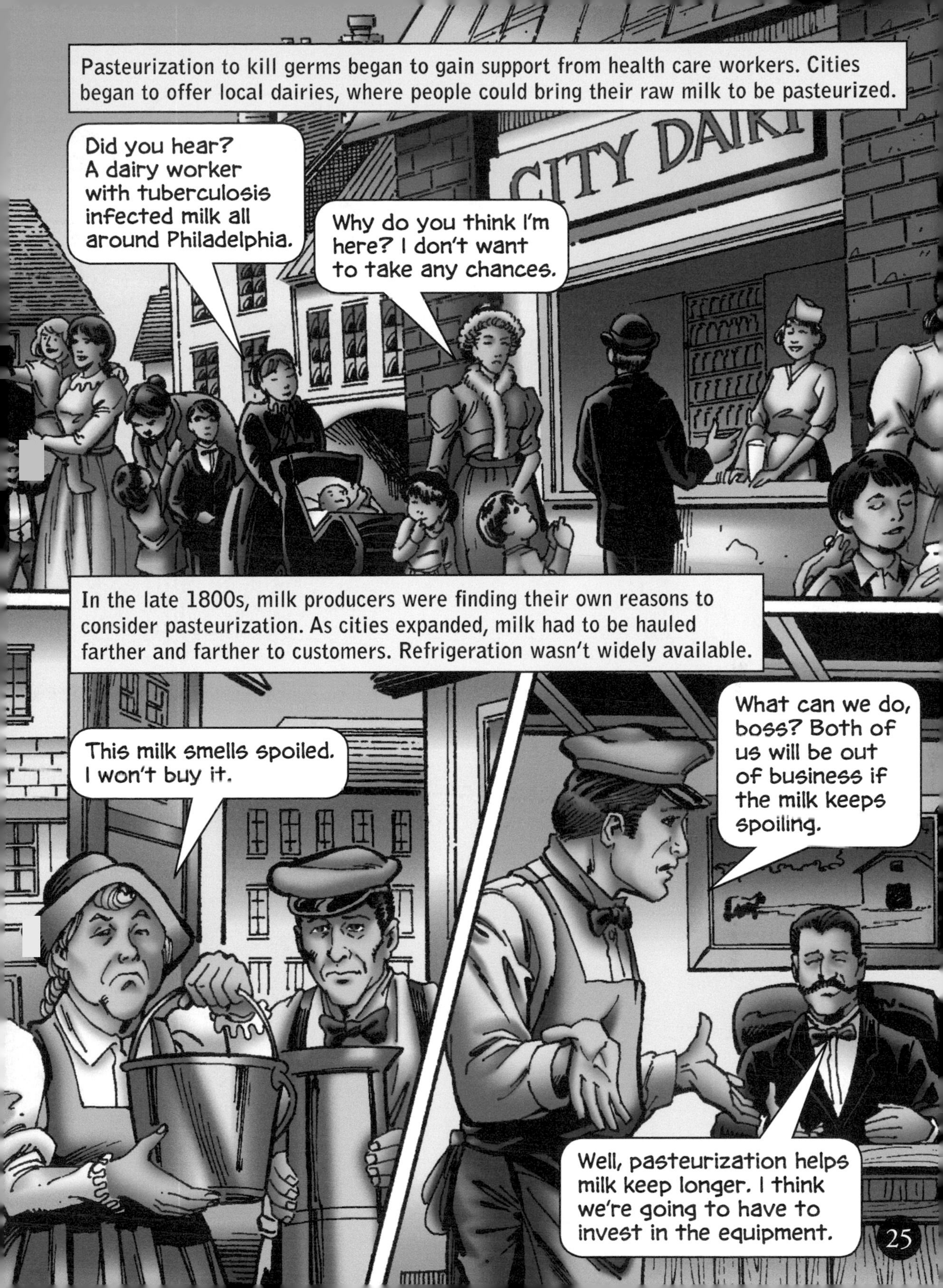
Pasteurization to kill germs began to gain support from health care workers. Cities began to offer local dairies, where people could bring their raw milk to be pasteurized.
CITY DAIRY
Did you hear? A dairy worker with tuberculosis infected milk all around Philadelphia.
Why do you think I'm here? I don't want to take any chances.
In the late 1800s, milk producers were finding their own reasons to consider pasteurization. As cities expanded, milk had to be hauled farther and farther to customers. Refrigeration wasn't widely available.
This milk smells spoiled. I won't buy it.
What can we do, boss? Both of us will be out of business if the milk keeps spoiling.
Well, pasteurization helps milk keep longer. I think we're going to have to invest in the equipment.

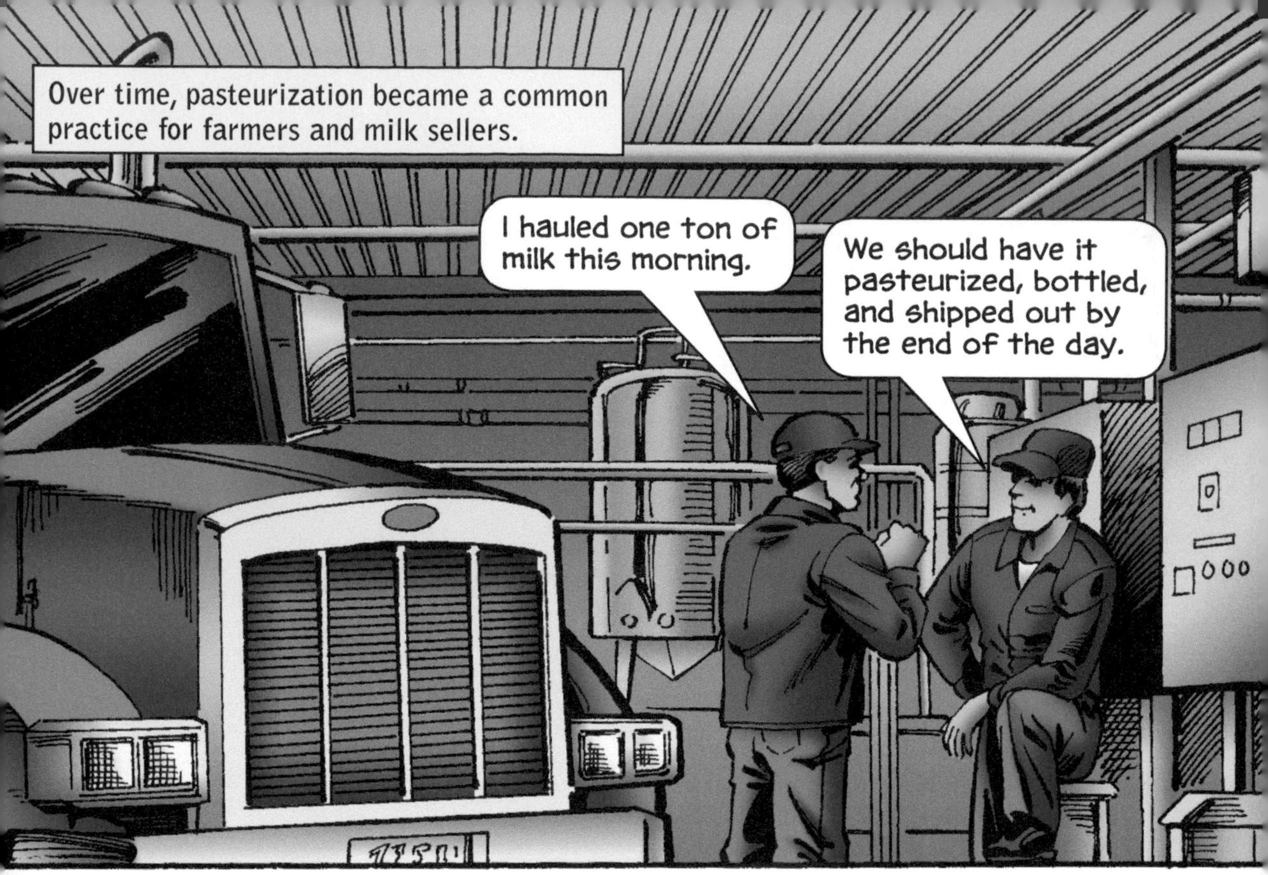
Over time, pasteurization became a common practice for farmers and milk sellers.
I hauled one ton of milk this morning.
We should have it pasteurized, bottled, and shipped out by the end of the day.

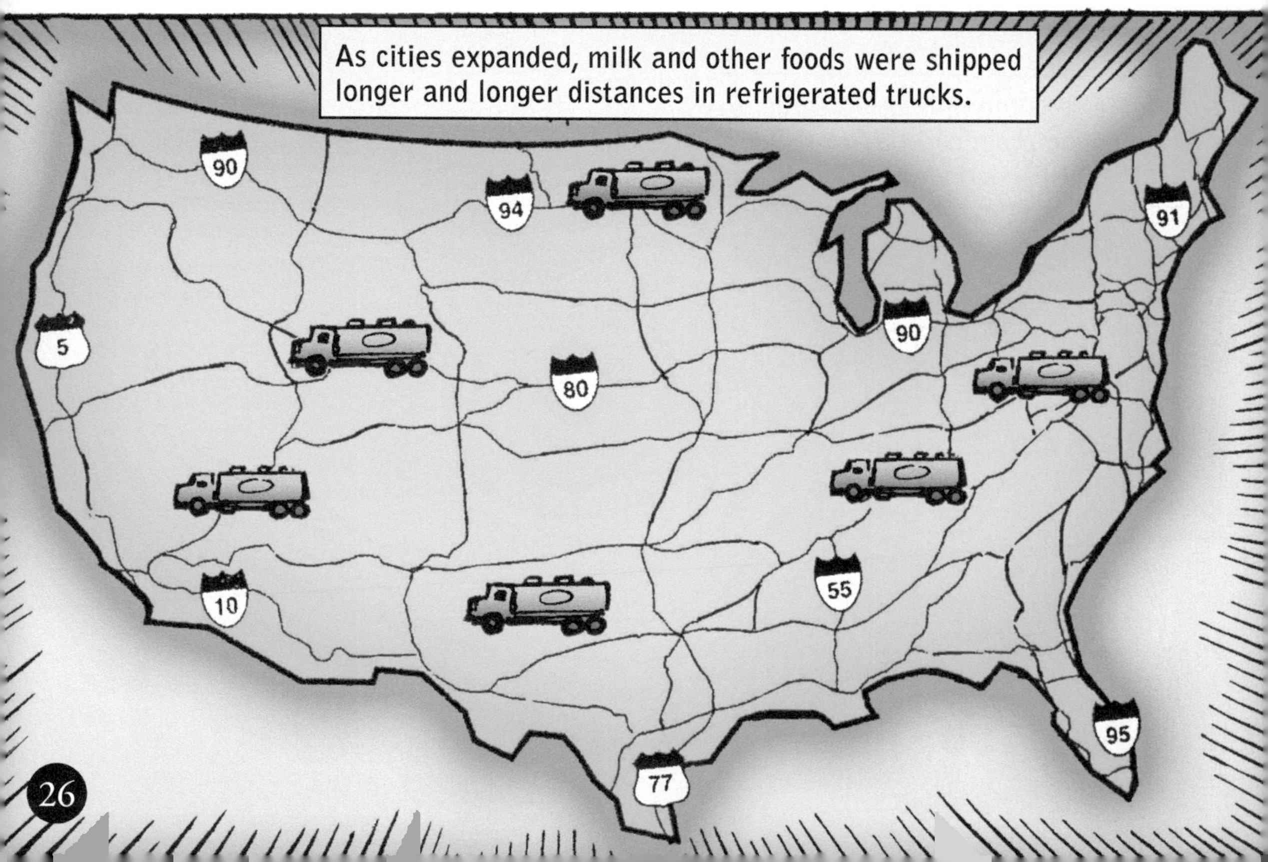
As cities expanded, milk and other foods were shipped longer and longer distances in refrigerated trucks.
90
94
91
5
90
80
10
55
95
77

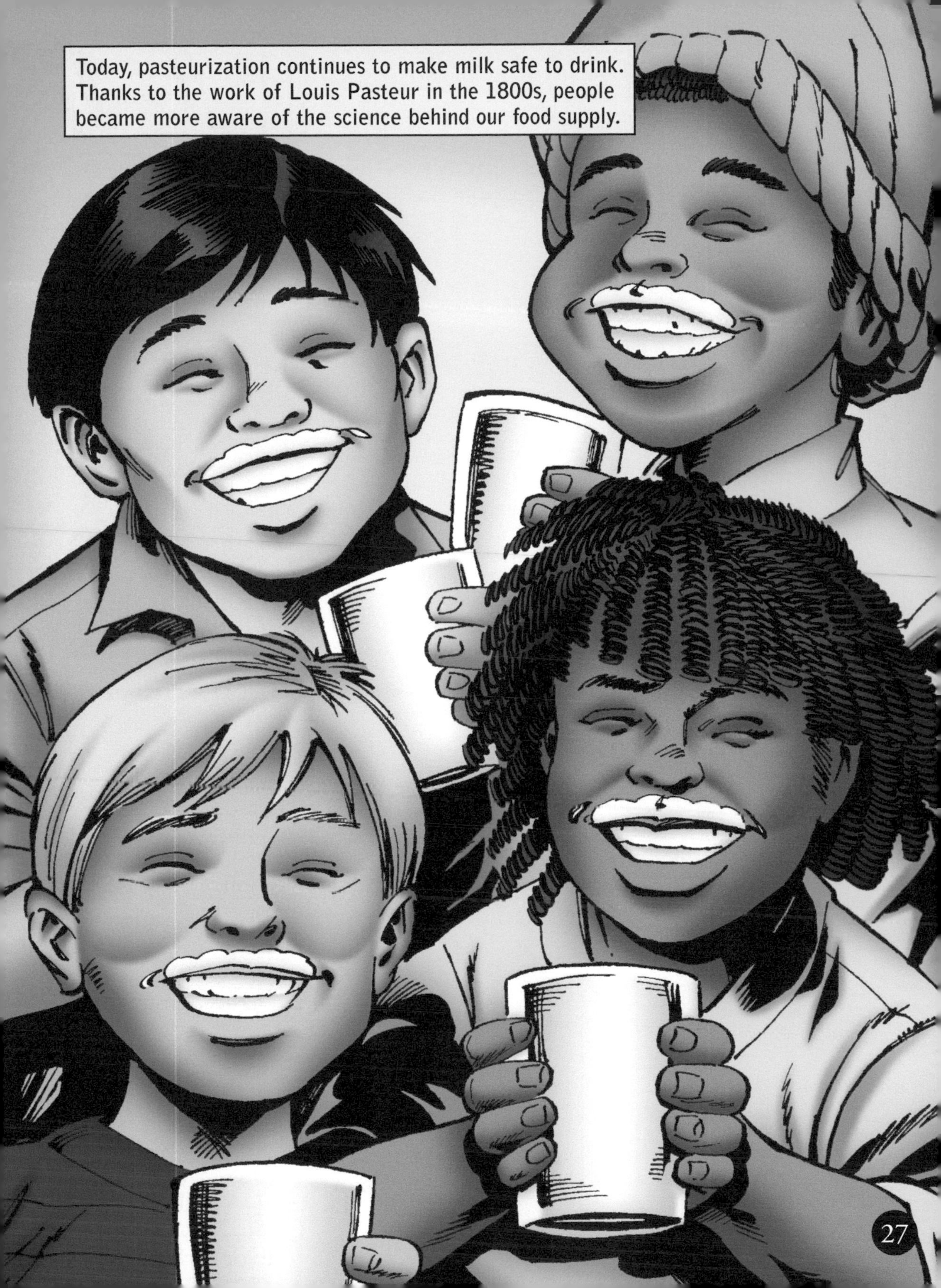
Today, pasteurization continues to make milk safe to drink. Thanks to the work of Louis Pasteur in the 1800s, people became more aware of the science behind our food supply.

MORE ABOUT
LOUIS PASTEUR
and
PASTEURIZATION

 Louis Pasteur was born in 1822 in France. He died in 1895. At the time of his death, he was considered a hero in France. The government ordered a state funeral, an honor usually given to a country's president or king. Many citizens joined the funeral procession in the streets of Paris.

 Pasteur and his wife Marie had five children, but only two lived past childhood. Two died of typhoid, a disease that attacks the intestines, while an unknown disease struck the other child. The deaths of his children motivated Pasteur to study diseases and learn to prevent them.

 Pasteur was very protective of his work. Even on vacation, Pasteur took his notebooks that contained the details of his experiments with him. He kept extremely detailed notes, numbering around 10,000 pages.

 Pasteurization helps kill bacteria that can show up in milk supplies. Some of the deadly diseases it can prevent are typhoid fever, tuberculosis, scarlet fever, and polio.

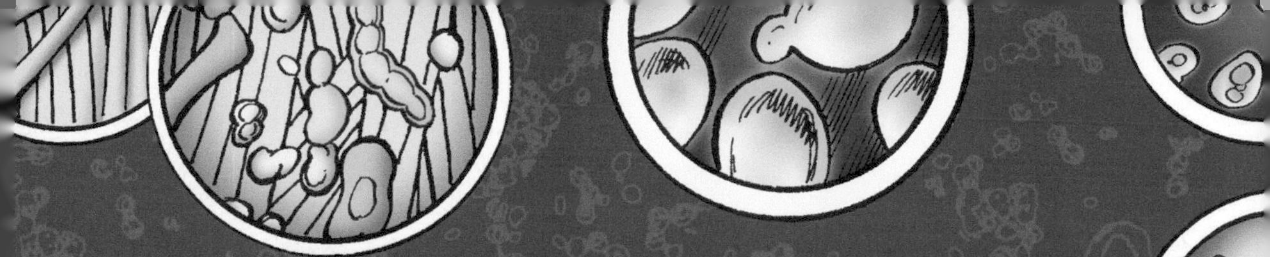

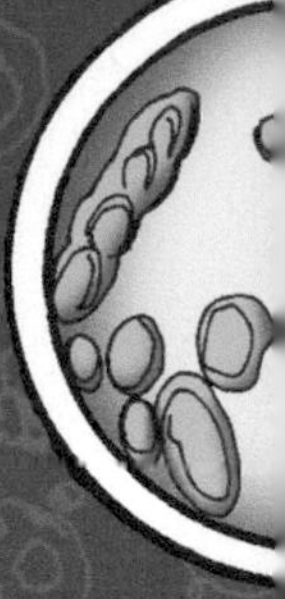

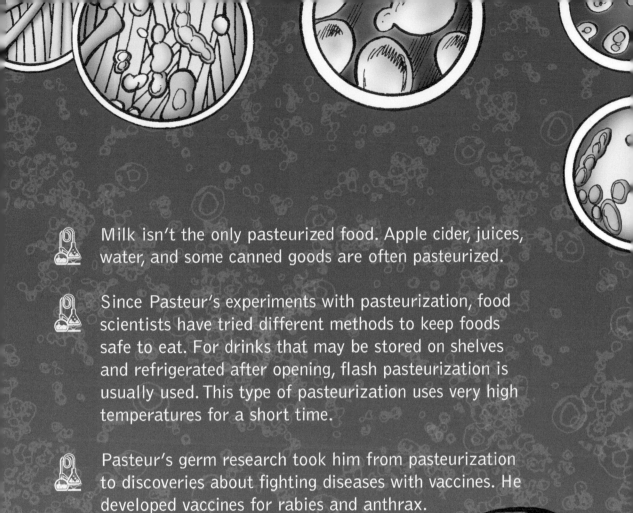

- Milk isn't the only pasteurized food. Apple cider, juices, water, and some canned goods are often pasteurized.

- Since Pasteur's experiments with pasteurization, food scientists have tried different methods to keep foods safe to eat. For drinks that may be stored on shelves and refrigerated after opening, flash pasteurization is usually used. This type of pasteurization uses very high temperatures for a short time.

- Pasteur's germ research took him from pasteurization to discoveries about fighting diseases with vaccines. He developed vaccines for rabies and anthrax.

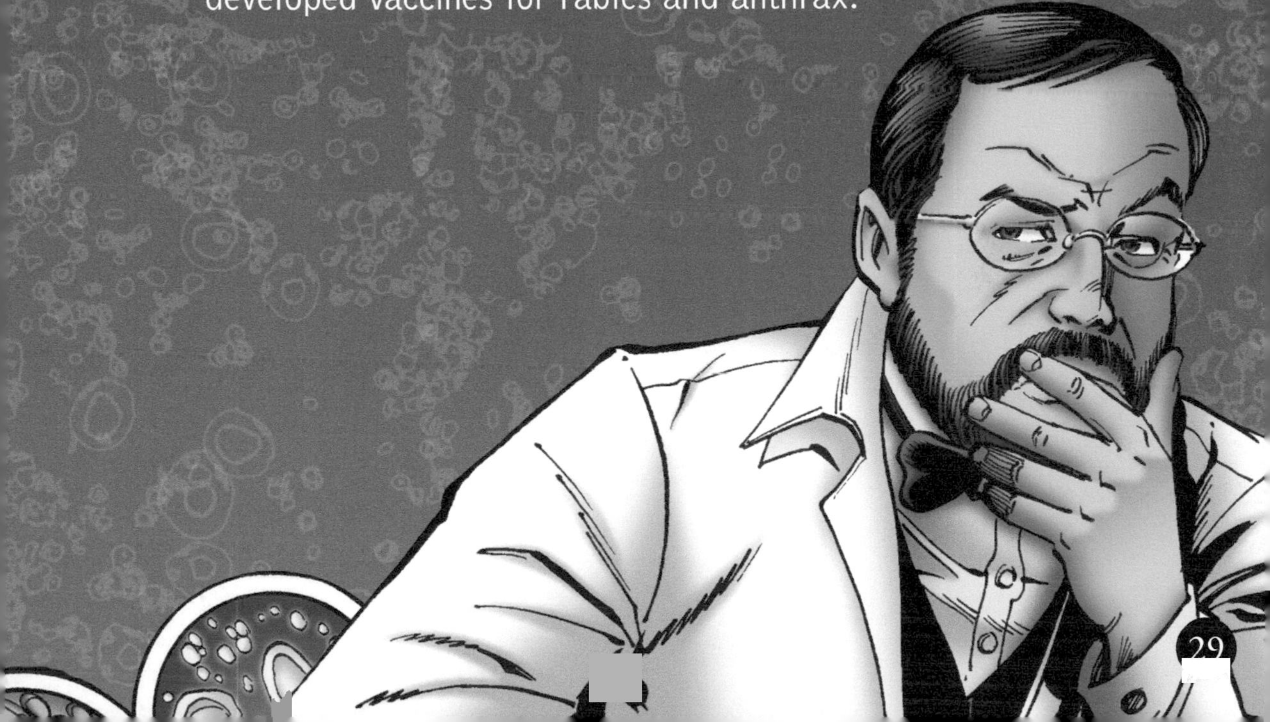

GLOSSARY

bacteria (bak-TIHR-ee-uh)—microscopic living things; some bacteria cause disease.

germ (JURM)—a microorganism; people usually use the word "germs" for microorganisms that make people sick.

microorganism (mye-kro-OR-gan-iz-um)—a living thing too small to be seen without a microscope

patent (PAT-uhnt)—a legal document that gives an inventor the right to make, use, or sell an invention for a set number of years

tuberculosis (tu-BUR-kyoo-low-sis)—a disease caused by bacteria that causes fever, weight loss, and coughing; left untreated, tuberculosis can lead to death.

yeast (YEEST)—a kind of microorganism called a fungus that causes dough to rise and alcohol to form

INTERNET SITES

FactHound offers a safe, fun way to find Internet sites related to this book. All of the sites on FactHound have been researched by our staff.

Here's how:
1. Visit *www.facthound.com*
2. Choose your grade level.
3. Type in this book ID **0736868445** for age-appropriate sites. You may also browse subjects by clicking on letters, or by clicking on pictures and words.
4. Click on the **Fetch It** button.

FactHound will fetch the best sites for you!

READ MORE

Fullick, Ann. *Louis Pasteur*. Groundbreakers. Chicago: Heinemann, 2001.

Isle, Mick. *Everything You Need to Know about Food Poisoning*. The Need to Know Library. New York: Rosen, 2001.

Nye, Bill. *Bill Nye the Science Guy's Great Big Book of Tiny Germs*. New York: Hyperion Books for Children, 2005.

Solway, Andrew. *What's Living in Your Kitchen?* Hidden Life. Chicago: Heinemann, 2004.

BIBLIOGRAPHY

Conant, James Bryant, ed. *Pasteur's Study of Fermentation*. Harvard Case Studies in Experimental Science. Cambridge, Mass.: Harvard University Press, 1952.

Debré, Patrice. *Louis Pasteur*. Baltimore: Johns Hopkins University Press, 1998.

Geison, Gerald L. *The Private Science of Louis Pasteur*. Princeton, N.J.: Princeton University Press, 1995.

Hall, Carl W., and G. Malcolm Trout. *Milk Pasteurization*. Westport, Conn.: Avi Publishing, 1968.

INDEX